‖‖ ‖ ‖‖‖‖‖ ‖ ‖ ‖‖ ‖‖‖‖ ‖‖‖‖‖‖‖ ‖‖ ‖‖

W9-BZW-174

Praise for *Magic in Plain Sight*

"A high five to Pat Heavren for crafting a powerful and poetic exploration of the state of *trust*. This is a thoughtful and eminently moving collection of teaching stories about the fine and fearsome art of accepting what is—whether it's our pain or our power—rather than struggling to change it or wrestle it into submission. This is a gift from a gifted teacher, and a brilliant student."

—Gregg Levoy, author of *Callings: Finding* and *Following an Authentic Life and Vital Signs: Discovering* and *Sustaining Your Passion For Life*

"This book opens doors and closes chapters; it discards judgments and invites inspiration. Bite-sized chunks of majestic wisdom are humbly delivered in seductively short stories about the ordinary and extraordinary. Do surrender to her words. Pat will hold you gently and sweetly, and better yet, you'll walk away with a steadier step, a wider smile, and a new take on reality."

—Elena V. Carpenter, former CEO, Four Winds Society

Pat Heavren's new book convincingly demonstrates the healing power of story. In reading these accounts of heartfelt insights and life-changing realizations, the struggle for wholeness is revealed as a messy and beautiful undertaking, returning us to what it means to be essentially human. All who value physical, emotional, and spiritual growth will be inspired by this compelling collection of stories that heal both inner and outer wounds.

—Robin Moore
author, storyteller, writing instructor

Magic

in

Plain Sight

Jessica~
May the magic around
you always be visible.

Gat Hemm

Magic

in

Plain Sight

When Acceptance Is the Healing

Patricia J. Heavren

Aldebaran Press

Copyright © 2017 by Patricia Heavren

All rights reserved. No part of this publication may be reproduced, distributed, or transmitted in any form or by any means, including photocopying, recording, digital scanning, or other electronic or mechanical methods, without the prior written permission of the publisher, except in the case of brief quotations embodied in critical reviews and certain other noncommercial uses permitted by copyright law.

For permission
requests, please address
Aldebaran Press
260 Amity Road, Suite 7
Woodbridge, Connecticut 06525

Published 2017 by Aldebaran Press
Printed in the United States of America

19 18 17   1 2 3 4

ISBN 978-0-9993746-0-3 (paperback)
ISBN 978-0-9993746-1-0 (ebook)

Library of Congress Control Number: 2017953967

This book is dedicated to Dr. Alberto Villoldo, founder of The Four Winds Society, in deep appreciation for the teachings that opened me to the wisdom, heart, and magic that were there all along.

TABLE OF CONTENTS

Part 3 *Complicated and Difficult Magic*

Foreword

Foreword. Forward. Four Words. "You need a shaman."

A shaman? Me? Three decades a practicing lawyer and law professor—I don't solve my problems through a shaman.

Or do I?

Arriving at Pat's office, I found out that shamans can wear jeans and a T-shirt and have offices next to a dentist. But the mystery and magic were there, along with the feathers, bells, stones, and sacred carvings, though Pat tells me she doesn't use the "sh" word to describe her work, understanding herself instead as a student of an enchanting presence she refers to as "living wisdom."

I was both nervous and excited. Through meditation, yoga, and extraordinary teachers, including Sue who recommended Pat to me, I felt that I was finally bringing together the dualities in my life: prayer and logic, faith and academic rigor, work at a university and my lifelong sense that intuition and heart far outweighed credential and achievement. But I still couldn't reconcile my programming from the womb and the loud voices that berated me when I stepped off the conventional paths at which I seemed to be excelling. "Lazy!" I heard, and cringed. "Selfish!" I heard, and cried. What bigger shame was there than to be lazy and selfish?

I dithered before scheduling an appointment with Pat and suddenly, I couldn't wait. If I could cope with, even silence, these voices somehow—how my life would change! I was sure of it.

But really? A shaman?

The morning of the appointment, Pat called in sick and asked to reschedule. I begged her, a stranger, to reconsider. She was kind and firm. "I really need all I have to do the work—I think we'll be better off if I recover."

And we were: In our first meeting, something huge instantly shifted. Pat listened carefully, then turned my story inside out, upside down, and sideways. She punned shamelessly, pointing my words right back at me. Most provocatively, she strongly and without hesitation asserted that laziness and selfishness were not only intrinsic to me and had been my whole life, but they were vital, honorable, true friends—perhaps my *best* friends. As I lay on her massage table, white became black, day became night, all was now true and possible.

She assigned me homework: to journal every day about the benefits of laziness and selfishness—to be grateful to them, to embrace and honor them. I was utterly confused and totally invigorated.

At the second meeting, she instantly noted that I looked excited and energized.

Ah, I thought, the chitchat rapport-building part of the professional interview—I've taught this a million times.

I explained that I'd come from teaching a class to law school students about managing the negative effects of

Vicarious Trauma, an occupational hazard in the lives of care and service providers for trauma survivors.

"Oh? How *do* you manage the negative effects?" Pat innocently asked.

"Mostly through intensified self-care, purposeful rest and restoration, you know," I casually answered.

The twinkle in Pat's eyes grew to flame. "You mean, by being lazy and selfish?"

Since that day, I have brought every intractable care and woe to Pat and I've never failed to leave utterly transformed. Old polarities are falling away. I see new possibilities in old relationships, new truths in old tropes, and new love in old pain. Pat's aliveness to the holy mystery literally in front of our faces infects my analysis of everything. What if this is a good thing? What if this "calamity" is the way forward? Like the saints and poets that the Stage Manager and Emily muse about in *Our Town*, Pat comes as close as she can to realizing life's wonder while she endeavors to live it—"every, every minute." No wonder she couldn't meet me the first time sick—she needs every sinew, cell, and molecule intact to live so bravely, fully in the moment. What valor it takes to offer this radical presence and follow it faithfully, even when she has no idea where it's heading!

And now, Pat has captured this enchantment in an intensely readable book. In these small glimpses into the living wisdom of her own and her client's stories, you too can experience the baffling, the thorny, the shattering and watch them yield, inexorably, to reverence, love, and hope. But this is not relentless optimism. Just when you think that everything always wraps in a bow, she shows that it doesn't; when you wonder if it's ever too much for her too, she reveals that it sometimes is. You'll ask yourself how she dares, and what she fears, and whether she sometimes just doesn't know either—then get her humble comical truths about all this too.

I hope you can see the twinkling smile, hear the awe-full punning, and feel your hair standing on end as revelation dawns—the insights you'll witness in this book are ever accompanied by utter delight, bliss, and indomitable impishness, all of which yield gold. Better than hard work, this is hard play, and Pat has the antic wisdom for all of it. If we're lucky, she'll write a second book about how to find the magic, everywhere, but even before she does, we find ourselves already changed, already listening differently, already awake, as Pat says, to the Garden of Eden in which we already live.

I remember leaving Pat's office one time and facing a doorway I had crossed hundreds of times. "Entrance," it read.

Or was it, en-trance?

Jean Koh Peters
Sol Goldman Clinical Professor of Law, Yale Law School
https://law.yale.edu/jean-koh-peters
July 2017

Introduction

This book was written in spite of me as much as because of me.

Maybe similar to you, I had no time to devote myself to epic-sized endeavors outside my ordinary routine. I had a business to run. I had children still living at home, family elders who needed support, relationships to keep alive, a body to be nurtured, and a house and garden to take care of. I had no savings that allowed me to take a sabbatical from my life to write, let alone fund a self-published book. Though I can manage a lot at one time, I'm not naturally given to efforts of rigorous self-discipline. Not a single circumstance in my life made this an easy task.

Luckily, it wasn't only up to me.

The book itself was my silent partner, a kind of Holy Ghostwriter. Its spirit rattled an invisible tin cup to finance the production of what you now hold in your hands or read on your screen. Also, like a magician who pulls a rabbit from a hat, it made time appear, necessary for the long walk in the desert that was the writing process.

The first hints that these pages planned to be my partner came many years ago at yoga teacher training when my cohort designated me "Most Likely to Write a Book." The last was when a stranger on a plane pointed me to speak with a friend who owned a company in Las Vegas ironically called Imagine Communications.

In the end, I simply played the role of surrogate mother for a cooperative and creative web of intelligence we can never fully understand and I could never describe, except perhaps by example—which brings us to the stories.

This book is a collection of twenty-five accounts of what happens when we shift our experience of the world by accepting what's present right in front of us. Challenging circumstances, disease, heartache, and whatever else we've been resisting, trying to make go away, become the vital ingredients in the unfolding of our greatest expression of *what is*. This gentle "death" of what could be or should be, or what we want or need to be, returns us to the essence of all possibilities. This is healing. And it's not about doing. It's directed only to the extent that it adapts in harmony to *what is* already. It's a co-creation for which no one can take credit. Every living expression contains a sacred seed waiting to be broken open with love.

Magic in plain view is what happens when that seed germinates and pushes up and out from the dark.

This book is a smorgasbord of parables, teaching stories, taken from sessions and programs with individuals, couples, and groups in my practice as an educator and co-creator, a "coach" working with others. Some are accounts from my own walk on the journey of the work. You can feast on them as a whole or sample them story-by-story to digest the magic rooted in each. If you're short on time and eager for transformation, the titles of each chapter dangle the magic right in front of you and provide a map of the path, one only you can traverse. Most importantly, try to move the living wisdom from the labyrinth of these chapters into your own life maze, so you can experience a direct encounter with amazement.

After all, no matter what your age, there's little, if any, time left to figure out how you want to live your life. If you're like me and the others whose stories are contained here, you've already overlooked far too much of the precious ordinary and spent way too long seeking inspiration, meaning, and value on the road to a better somewhere else.

We're part of a bright, mysterious web that stretches wide and is connected well beyond what we can ever fathom on our own. All we need to do is accept, and bring love to what is there.

Author's Note

All the stories here are shared with permission; some names have been changed, some not. Dialogue and details have been re-shaped from memory and present-moment imagining and are based on how the story lived in the author at the time of its writing.

Just like life.

Patricia J. Heavren

"This world we are born into—this complicated, difficult, hauntingly touching world—is the one whole thing. It is the world we awaken in, and awaken to.

Our awakening is made of this world, just as it is.

It doesn't come from some other realm like a bolt from the blue, and you don't go to someplace else when you awaken.

Awakening is not a destination, and meditation is not a bus ride.

Awakening is the unfolding of an ability to see what has always been here. To see, more and more reliably, what is actually in front of you."

—*Joan Sutherland*

Part 1

Hauntingly Touching Magic

Chapter 1

Erase the Dividing Line, Except When You Need It

Out beyond ideas of wrongdoing and rightdoing,
there is a field. I'll meet you there.

When the soul lies down in that grass,
the world is too full to talk about.
Ideas, language, even the phrase *each other*
doesn't make any sense.

From *The Essential Rumi,* by Coleman Barks

used with permission

❧

"Find a partner," one of the facilitators said. "When you do, draw an invisible line between the two of you and each take a turn trying to get the other to cross over to your side."

This was the icebreaker exercise that introduced the forty-hour certificate training, Mediation and Conflict Resolution, held on the campus of the new law school at our local university. My attendance was a foray down a dark alley, coming some months after leaving a long-time executive job in non-profit management and before my dive into healing and neo-shamanic studies, which landed me in my next career as a mediator of a different kind.

When I left my position, I was at the top of my game, successful and well-regarded in the field. Yet some inner guidance system, a gnawing in my gut I couldn't dismiss, led me to resign. I wasn't unhappy. I'd just become too comfortable. Some instinct knew I needed to do something more. The fact that my husband didn't have a job yet after finishing graduate school and we had three small mouths to feed couldn't quell the sense of adventure that called out to me from a dark somewhere else.

The space on the law-school campus where the mediation training was held was in the shadow of a mountain shaped liked a sleeping giant looming on the other side of the picture windows. The room appeared to me as an alternate reality, an entirely different universe than I was accustomed to. The group was mostly composed of attorneys expanding their skills to meet the growing demand for non-adversarial, collaborative alternatives to handling personal, business, and community disputes. Other attendees came from human-resource, civil-service, and advocacy backgrounds.

Besides the lone ombudsman, I was the odd one out with no affiliation or title.

Or so it appeared.

In hindsight, I see it was both true and not true. I was different from and the same as everyone else. Though I traveled on the margin of this particular group, we were all in the shadow of that sleeping giant together, looking for a fresh perspective in our work. We were like immigrants from various cultures docked at an Ellis Island disguised as an oversized conference table. We came to cultivate the ability to listen carefully and become powerful meeting points between foreign and often unfriendly points of view.

In this law school setting, Lady Liberty was replaced by a blindfolded Lady Justice holding a scale and sword rather than a torch.

Looking around for a partner for the icebreaker, my eyes caught the gaze of a friendly guy I'd talked to earlier. He'd recently completed his law degree and was looking to open a family-law practice.

"You go first, Don," I said, taking a few steps back from the imagined line between us.

"Okay. So, Pat, um … why don't you come on over here to my side of the line? You look a little lonely over there."

I smiled tolerantly at what sounded to both of us like a lame pickup line.

"Well, it's a great view from over here. But I don't think you can really see what I see from where you're standing." Don glanced left and right with an exaggerated look of marvel on his face. "In fact, it's so wonderful on this side, you simply *have* to see it from my perspective." This time he punctuated the request by holding out his hand. I thought he was about to grab me and pull me across the imaginary line.

At that moment, my whole body began to register what was happening.

Everything Don said indicated that he was in a better place than I was. For him, it was true that it *was* an extraordinary view from his side of the line. But he never once offered to catch a view from where I was before trying to convince me that what *he* saw was way more desirable than what *I* saw.

It was clear that Don and I had tapped into some larger fault line that ran beneath all our feet all the time. I let myself open to the impressions that began to shake up from beneath the floor, then dug in my heels.

"You know, Don, I'm happy that you like life on your side of the line. But I like it over here. I may pay you a visit one day, but right now I don't want to give up what I have."

After a few seconds, I added, "And Don? Honestly, I think you're the one missing out."

Despite Don's apparent sincerity, conceding to him meant leaving my favored position. His gain felt like my loss, no matter what. After I showed no sign of giving in, Don gave up.

Something profound was stirring below this playful surface and we paused for a break, walking through the room for a few minutes to see what was going on with the other partners.

All sorts of negotiations, from half-comic to serious, were occurring between our classmates, employing every possible twist in their bids for peacekeeping and resolution in this simple icebreaker exercise. Attendees were obviously taking advantage of permission to act in exaggerated ways they usually suppressed. One man pulled a wallet out of his suit jacket pocket and tried to bribe his partner across the line.

Even a little lighthearted brawl erupted, a tug of war gone awry. It was as if memories from their own participation in or witnessing of conflicts were ripe and ready to take over at the first hint of invitation.

But the truth was that entire continental divides of human history lay behind these ancient stories, icy hills of habit stored in the collective DNA in the room. Mostly it came down to this: We don't like to give things up. We're as seemingly unmovable as mountains.

I found myself wondering something as Don and I strolled the room together watching our counterparts. *What would start the ice caps finally melting? Nobody wants to give anything up, not even in playacting, no matter how skillful the facilitation of concessions is presented or offered. Without addressing this, "resolutions" to conflict were about as long lasting as the kind we make on New Year's Eve.*

When my partner and I stepped back together for my turn at the task, I didn't have a plan. Nothing clever had occurred to me. Yet I was aware that something was bubbling to the surface and wanted to see what would emerge if I got really quiet and didn't let my mind plot a response to this incredible personal and collective dilemma. So I asked Don if he minded if I closed my eyes for a bit.

I opened them a minute or so later and put my hand in my pretend back pocket, taking out something invisible. I dropped into a squat and rubbed it in a zigzag over the highly polished wood floor in the space between us. I stood up, placed the mimed object back where it came from, and smiled across at Don.

"What was *that*?" he asked with a dumbfounded expression and a slight scrunch to his nose, even as he tried to maintain his best bridge-builder tone.

"Well," I said after a careful pause to select my words, still trying to digest my own response, "we drew an imaginary line together, didn't we? So I just took out an imaginary eraser and erased the imaginary line."

"Oh," was all Don managed beyond the dubious expression on his face.

I left it at that, as the facilitator was already calling us back to take our seats. At the same time, I glanced out the window to see if the sleeping giant was beginning to rouse.

I didn't tell Don that since there was no actual line, we were both exactly where we were and wanted to be. Nothing divided us. We didn't have to move an inch. We didn't have to give up anything to see, empathize with, and appreciate each other. We could share the whole space and embrace and be grateful for our varied perspectives. At home everywhere, we were no longer immigrants—no need to protect our turf or fear Border Patrol.

Just before we sat back down, Don gave me what became my first conscious memory of *the look*.

Until that icebreaking exercise, I'd hidden most of what I saw from all but a select few in an attempt to fit in, to quell a long and enduring loneliness that came from glimpsing extraordinary landscapes while living smack dab in the middle of an ordinary world. I had a strong intimation that *the look* would be generated again (and again) by my wanderings into the new world I sensed ahead.

At the end of forty student hours filled with tips, tools, and role-plays of mediating real-life conflicts, the co-facilitators held one-on-one meetings with each of us who participated in the program. When it was my turn for the exit interview with the facilitators, the icebreaker leader turned to me. "Did you get what you came for?"

"Honestly? I have no idea," I replied. "I'm not sure I'm meant to be a professional mediator, but there is one thing I'm certain about. I'll be back one day to innovate the field. I can't tell you why or how, but I just know it's true."

The words escaped before I had the time to push the edit button, but as soon as they came out of my mouth, a hot blush spread across my cheeks. I was utterly embarrassed. I felt horribly egotistical and riddled with shame, while simultaneously sensing what I said was completely true. I was years from learning how to bring a little light and love to my dark and judgmental ego.

The response from the co-facilitators was predictable. I received *the look* from both of them, for the second time in one week.

To hide my embarrassment, I quickly offered my planned and sincere thank you for learning a lot and enjoying the program tremendously. I didn't mention to them that most of what I got happened for me in the first ten minutes during the icebreaker exercise, that some glacial divide had begun to melt. Later, I'd realize the same was true when a client sat down in front of me and we broke the ice with conversation.

As I shook hands with the facilitators and the large intimidating door closed behind me, I thought of Lady Justice and her blindfold. It cut off her vision outward, but focused it inward, and perhaps allowed the all-seeing eye, the third eye mythically located in the midbrain along with the corpus callosum, to emerge. The corpus callosum was the mediator between the left and right hemispheres of the brain, after all.

As I walked to my car, I reflected on how the most interesting experiences for me came as calls from the dark rather than a beckoning from the light. Leaving the comfort zone of my job was one, taking this course was another. It was an awesome call—a "call-awesome."

I laughed quietly to myself. *I was* the callosum, the mediator between the worlds. I now carried a certificate from a law school to prove it.

Blindfold officially off, I drove through the marble-and-brick gateway of the campus and onto the stretch of road that hugged the side of the mountain. As I drove, I watched the gold line painted down the middle, dividing the traffic flow on the busy street.

There was still at least one line that I wouldn't be erasing.

Chapter 2

Trust Everything

Emily was one of the first people to walk through my office door. Her life had been curtailed by the agoraphobia and rapidly declining health of her older husband Gordon. He was dependent on her to the point where she felt she was losing touch with what sustained her. She exhibited all the signs of a caregiver under tremendous strain.

"The support groups are okay on one level, but not terribly helpful," she recounted as she listed the things she was doing for herself at the recommendation of her therapist. "Talking about it doesn't seem to really shift anything. Sometimes I feel more discouraged by being around others who are in the same situation. It seems like another thing I have to do—provide support for them, while I'm drowning myself."

Emily and I first met the day she slipped a note into my coat when I was walking out of church. While I knew her name and that she often sat with her husband a few rows behind us during the service, the seventy-something woman with the boldly dyed, spikey hair was mostly a stranger.

That particular Sunday, Emily came up beside me with a quick hello. I had no hands free. I was holding our youngest child with one arm, while my husband and I corralled our two older children through the zigzag of cars lined up to leave the parking lot. So she placed the folded piece of paper into my jacket pocket.

When I got to our car, I reached for the curiously delivered note. Emily had scribbled a few sentences of encouragement that she obviously thought I needed, a reminder to take as good care of myself as I appeared to be doing with our children. So it was ironic when, more than a few years later, she made her way through the doorway of my newly opened office to look to me for a similar sort of support.

"While words can often be really helpful, sometimes they do fall short," I said, responding to her experience in the support groups. "So let's try something else. I'm going to get quiet and close my eyes and maybe search for something present in the story you're telling me about your life with Gordon. Sound good?" I didn't wait for a direct reply. The fact that she was present was the permission.

A few minutes after closing my eyes, something appeared in my view. A cloaked figure stood in front of me and handed me an apple and a silver cheese grater.

I'm in trouble, I thought. *Just what the hell am I supposed to do with this?* But then I recalled the voice of my teacher, who had instructed us to always trust the impressions we received when journeying on another person's behalf.

To my surprise, the cloaked figure beamed a message back, as if I were addressing my question to him, or her, or it, rather than myself. That is, if any difference between him-her-it and me existed in the first place. The witness consciousness in me was already having a field day with what was happening.

Tell her to use them together.

Well, thanks, but that's not much help, I responded in this speechless dialogue I was suddenly having with a faceless figure that simultaneously seemed to appear both outside and inside of me. *You're not the one charging a fee for this.*

I couldn't believe I was actually arguing with an apparition.

With thoughts of losing all the credibility I'd built in the successful sessions with my first dozen clients, I opened my eyes and looked into what I perceived as Emily's way-too-hopeful gaze. I walked over to her, lightly blew the two images I was given by the cloaked figure into her heart center, and sat down. She looked exhausted, in desperate need of hearing something that would somehow turn her world around, and I hated the idea that I was about to disappoint her. But like a dutiful student, I followed the instructions of my teacher.

"So, Emily. Sometimes things arise and we don't immediately recognize their value," I began, already planning my escape route out of a situation that I suspected was about to end badly. "Uh, so, I just delivered an apple and a cheese grater into the heart center of the energetic field around you. I'm supposed to tell you to take the apple and grater and use them together," I said as quickly as I could to hide the wince behind my words. I didn't mention that the instruction came from a cloaked and hooded figure. I had to preserve what little dignity I had left in the face of what I expected was about to be an onslaught of judgment.

But if Emily sensed the doubt I was holding, she was having none of it. Instead, she took what I said utterly seriously and closed her own eyes. I watched her. After several minutes, she raised both hands. Holding one still, she moved the other repetitively up and down. It didn't take long for her to drop her hands and open her eyes. Tears were streaming down her face. "It's my Greater Core, Pat. You've returned me to my Greater Core."

I nodded in silent agreement, but I was thinking, *I did what?*

Though I appeared to be agreeing with her, I couldn't process what was happening. I knew I had to catch up to Emily, who appeared to be way *way* ahead of me. At the same time, part of my mind was taking notes: Always trust what's present. It's never about retrieving something you're missing. It's about remembering what you've had all along and forgotten. It was very Dorothy in the Wizard of Oz.

"It was right there. So very exciting," Emily gushed. "I did exactly what you said. They needed to be used together, so I held an imaginary apple in one hand and the grater in the other … until … and then … there it was! I kept grating the apple until I was holding my Greater Core again. Pat, in a way it makes so much sense. I was just saying yesterday at the support group that Gordon's needs and demands have made me feel weary to my core. I guess his illness has been guiding me to find this all along," she added, exposing a whole other dimension of the healing.

I wondered if some essence of Gordon had been under the cloak and hood, but definitely kept that thought to myself.

I pretended not to be shocked, even though I was, as if this happened all the time in the freshly painted office for which I'd recently signed a lease. I hadn't even finished taking all the certification classes. I was, in fact, the inexperienced healer people were sometimes warned about seeing. I was also operating from the premise of the famous

line from *Field of Dreams,* "If you build it, they will come."
And here, one of my first clients had already become my
advanced teacher, bestowing on me an early and important
gift about what the business of healing really meant, by
adding another piece to my invisible operating plan: "If you
trust, it's already there."

After talking for a while about how to integrate her
experience when she returned home, Emily stood up,
hugged me tightly, and left a check for triple my newly set
fee on the table next to her chair.

I couldn't take it in as a newbie practitioner, even as
my confidence in the work began to grow and continued to
prove itself valuable to others time after time. In the early
years of my practice, I was fearful of becoming someone in
whom others placed their absolute trust and confidence to
change them, knowing already that those who came were
doing their own healing. I was deeply afraid that my clients
would give their power to me and surrender the wisdom of
their own intuitive voices. It took seven or eight years of
practice to overcome the idea that my client as the healer
was good and me as the healer was bad. Though I was successful in my practice, I was also filled with caution about
my own power. I hadn't yet developed a relationship with
ego as being another expression of the One. I kept trying to
keep it in check.

Eventually, finally, I was able to look back and recognize another layer of treasure in the words Emily offered
both of us that day: I *did* have a role in the experience of her
remembering who she was at her core.

Without me, it couldn't have unfolded for her quite
that way, though it certainly could have in another. It was
simply what happened. Without Emily, who knows how

long it would have taken me to see value in trusting what I heard when I listened. I needed her—and all the others who followed—as much as they seemed to need me.

What we refer to as healing or sacred remembering is always a co-creation. Trust and openness are key. Even, or perhaps especially, when circumstances are presented in a cloak of mystery or challenge or … absurdity.

Chapter 3
See Wisdom Through Old Eyes

"He is saying the past is in front of us and the future is behind us. We are not able to see what is coming, which is why the future is behind." The translator, Odon, spoke excellent English—dressed in a Spanish accent.

The sentence pierced me like the direct hit of an arrow. It traveled the same trajectory as the line of light that gleamed from Don Mariano's right eye when he smiled a wide grin, exposing two gaps on either side of his crooked front teeth. Feathered lines scratched out from the edges of his eyes to his temples, marking his smile in decades of time in the same way rings mark the age of a cut tree.

Don Mariano lived high in the Andes of Peru, in a village even now accessible to the modern world only by primitive road. As recently as his early childhood, the passage up and down the mountain was rarely traversed.

Since the Spanish conquest of the 1500s, the people of Q'eros lived apart from the developing world, having fled Cusco, known as the City of Gold, and the Europeans who came to claim its treasures. It wasn't until the early to mid-twentieth century that their culture began to slowly move down the mountain, like the glaciers spoken of in their prophecies, said to mark the beginning of a time of great change.

Now the path had become a kind of Silk Road, with cell phones making their way up the mountain, while teachings made their way back down, linking the two worlds. The modern one was as hungry for ancient wisdom as the grandchildren of this indigenous cultural enclave were for Facebook.

And so we sat that day, members of two vastly different cultures, ironically assembled in a Veterans of Foreign Wars hall in the northeastern U.S. In a way, we represented present-day VFW survivors, foreigners in our own lands looking to bring divided worlds together. We were driven to exchange, desiring to join the common treasures and unique expressions of cultural wisdom to support the global good.

The only small conquest here was overcoming the linguistic barrier, as Quechua itself was a dying language.

As Don Mariano Quispe Flores spoke, Odon leaned forward with folded hands, elbows propped on knees. His head nodded slightly as he listened and translated, sometimes asking a clarifying question. He exhibited a subtle but obvious devotion to his teacher that went well beyond the respectful attention afforded a mentor by a mentee. He clearly loved him.

At one point, Odon looked up at the few of us gathered and offered the idea about the past being ahead of us and the future behind that pierced me open.

So today is the result of how yesterday's experience lives within us, I thought. *No wonder our collective fondness for marching courageously forward often walks us into a continual repeat of history. And what he's also saying is that the future is behind us where we can't see it. How different an approach*

*that is from what makes the North American world tick in its
drive to see and plan for a willfully desired future, rather than
to work with it as a supportive, unknowable force.*

I wasn't startled so much by the concept, which immediately rang true as something I already knew. It was the
backwards jolt of it that upended me, catapulting me from
a familiar orientation to its reverse.

Perhaps everything I thought was true could be exactly
the opposite.

As the metaphoric arrow of his words hit me between
the eyes, I thought of the retina, how it receives light as
it enters through the lenses of the eyes, recording what
the eyes see both backwards and upside down. The retina
converts the light into neural signals that are forwarded to
various visual centers and ultimately to the neo-cortex, the
area of the brain responsible for recognizing what appears
in front of us.

While many processes influence the recognition of
what's observed, one thing is certain: No two of us see
what's "out there" in the exact same way. Everything is sub-
jective; there is no true objective reality apart from the one
constructed by each unique seer, just close approximations
of consensual agreement that we identify and commonly
refer to as "reality." And given the way the stories of human
history are often held with disdain and bitterness, it's no
wonder our world has assembled the way it has today.

With the pulling back of an invisible bow and the
whistling release of low spoken words in an ancient foreign
language, Don Mariano exposed the sheer and utter malle-
ability of the phenomenal world.

And since that's so, it's time to tell the stories of what
we see as expressions of love, to create a new world.

Chapter 4

See Wisdom Through New Eyes

When the memory of her brother Robert arose out of the blue, Bernadette was sitting on a stool at a granite countertop, drinking a cup of coffee and picking at a muffin, while writing what she refers to as her "morning pages" in her journal.

I walked into the kitchen in the house in suburban New Jersey a couple of hours before the others would join us there for a weekend-long program I was leading.

"It's strange," Bernadette said in her hallmark New York accent as I reached to fill my own empty coffee cup. "I don't know why, but something has *really* come up for me around my brother this morning."

She thought it all had been put to rest. It had been more than twenty-five years since her beloved younger brother died of AIDS and she told me that this morning, for some reason, her heart ached again with a memory that haunted her. "I didn't hold or physically touch him the last time I saw him, on his deathbed."

I wondered if her morning pages were really *mourning* pages, evidence of an ever-turning cycle that sought a different ending to lead to a new beginning. Over breakfast, she began to tell me the story.

When Bernadette's brother was born, she was thirteen. Her older brother Charlie was eighteen. There was a significant age difference among the three siblings, but particularly between Robert and Charlie.

Bernadette's mother struggled with mental-health issues throughout her life, but particularly just after Robert's birth, probably some form of post-partum depression that exacerbated her usual challenges. Her mom was unable to fully care for Robert. As a result, she relied on her daughter to step in as a sort of surrogate. It was a role Bernadette welcomed. As a result, she and Robert grew up extraordinarily close and remained so after she, and eventually he, moved out of their family home. In many ways, he was more like a son than a brother to her.

"Early on, I knew Robert was gay, perhaps even before he did."

As he grew older, she introduced him to friends of hers who were also gay, helping him bridge his emerging awareness of self to a new community. She also supported his creative path as a talented visual artist. As Robert matured into young adulthood, their relationship intensified.

When Robert was in his mid-twenties, Bernadette received a call from his roommate. He told her he was worried, because Robert had become quite ill. She went to see her brother immediately. When she arrived, Bernadette knew at first glance that something was terribly wrong; her suspicion was confirmed by the doctor Bernadette took Robert to see, who diagnosed him with AIDS. In the early 1980s, this news was tantamount to a death sentence. It was a time when not only little was known about HIV infection and transmission, but also a cloud of paranoia hovered over the crisis.

Bernadette provided emotional support and all kinds of care for Robert during his illness. Her husband was supportive of Bernadette helping Robert, though he made one request during the weeks and months of his illness: that she refrain from any close physical contact with Robert, including hugging him.

Later, in the group, I asked Bernadette to share what she had with me about the ghosts of guilt and regret that had been knocking at her door since early morning. I sensed she needed something from the others. From her seat in the leather chair next to the fire, she recounted Robert's final moments in great detail.

"The guilt was the worst the last time I saw him. We could all tell he was near the end. We were at the hospital and I was standing in front of Robert's bed." She raised her hand in front of her as if to point out the visual she was seeing in her mind's eye. "My mother was on the left side and Charlie was on the right. My husband, who had never come to the hospital before, was behind me. A priest came in and administered Robert's last rites, which was very comforting for my mother, who was a devout Catholic." Bernadette paused here with a faraway look in her eyes, the gas flames of the fireplace dancing behind her before continuing.

"I looked at Robert thinking it was time for him to go—there was nothing here for him anymore—when I saw Charlie putting on a pair of rubber gloves. He then reached over Robert and began to gently and lovingly rub his back. After a long while, as Robert seemed to be holding steady, we made the difficult decision to go home. We weren't gone long before I got the call from the hospital that Robert had passed.

I was devastated on so many levels—not the least of which was that I never hugged him. I could have just held him in my arms and told him how much I loved him. But I didn't. I wanted to honor the promise I'd made to my husband."

Everyone in the room listened intently.

Her voice dropped to a whisper. "I've held onto that guilt for many, many years." Small tears rolled from Bernadette's eyes.

"Bernadette," I asked gently, "can we bring your story alive?"

She looked at me and nodded, the emotion invisibly gripping her by the throat. I could tell she was unsure of the invitation I was offering. I was uncertain, too. I had no idea what would unfold.

"Let's recreate the scene in your brother's hospital room and look at it again … together. Are you willing?"

She nodded. I knew she not only trusted me, but she trusted everyone present. While the group had been together for only two meetings, its members were unusually bonded.

I asked Bernadette to pick someone to role-play Robert and the others who were present with her brother at the time of his death. She did this while circling the room: first choosing "Robert," then the characters of "Mom," "Charlie," and "her husband." When she finished reconfiguring living room to hospital room, I physically turned Bernadette to face me.

As she did, I asked her if she was willing to step back into the scene and tell me what she saw *now*. I asked the group to remember Bernadette's story and, without words, to silently follow the "script" she had provided in her narration to us just a few minutes before.

I led Bernadette to the spot closest to the door in the room and positioned her in front of her surrogate husband. Then I turned her to take the long view of Robert's deathbed.

"Bernadette, trust the memory preserved here. It contains everything you need to see in it for healing. We don't need to change anything. All you need to do is bring an empty mind, a new pair of eyes, a fresh perspective."

Then I leaned back and whispered to the man playing Bernadette's husband to quietly repeat this phrase aloud, "Don't touch him … Don't hug him ... Don't touch him."

I stood by Bernadette, not knowing what would happen, but continuing to trust that something would. As if on cue, "Charlie" put on imaginary gloves and, as gently and lovingly as Bernadette described a few minutes before, began rubbing Robert's back.

The room was still. It went on for a full minute before tears began to roll down Robert's face.

"Keep watching, Bernadette," I said softly.

Soon what was unconscious, what had been living beneath the surface for twenty-five years yearning to be seen differently, was brought alive in the room. Alongside the gentle chant of her husband's words—"*Bernadette, don't touch him, don't hug him …*" repeating in intermittent skips like a needle stuck in the groove of an instructive rather than cautionary record—the awareness landed.

And it landed big; everyone could feel it. We watched it wash from the top of Bernadette's head to the bottom of her feet. The downward tsunami took twenty-five years of guilt along with it.

Bernadette saw what she couldn't see years before. Robert knew all along, starting on the day he was born, how much his sister loved him. By keeping the promise she made to her husband, Robert and Charlie were able to connect at Robert's deathbed in a way they never had during the whole of their lives, due to the great generational gap and other differences they never crossed until Robert's final moments.

Bernadette realized how perfect it was, *as it was.*

The scene continued. The play-acting Robert's tears dropped out of the edges of his eyes and down to the carpeted floor. Charlie was visibly moved. Though this part wasn't in Bernadette's original script, it was now. The two men from the group who were living this re-creation of her story were suddenly consumed by it. In that moment, they moved from within and beyond her story and embraced each other, both quietly crying.

Everyone in the room was moved. We were sharing a field of experience that belonged to all of us.

I understood in that moment that it was this way with everything. If we're willing to go deep enough into what we encounter right in front of us, adding nothing and taking nothing away, we often discover that the darkest and most limiting possibilities carry the seed of greatest healing—a healing that is already present, with the capacity to unfold an entirely new reality.

It proved what I knew already, that when we connect into a state of harmonious ever-presence, the consciousness of it naturally extends to the environment around us. I was watching it unfold in the room as if Bernadette's experience sparked a living game of dominos.

A short time later when the actors returned to their seats, each person shared his and her unique perspective. They all reported receiving *pings* to their own pasts, ricocheting off what lived hidden in their own buried depths.

What surfaced was amazing.

"Robert," still on the floor, lost his own uncle to AIDS at around the same time Bernadette's brother died; what's more, he himself was also gay and, as it turned out, he shared with the group he was HIV positive, though the infection was no longer detectable in his blood.

"Charlie" reported a deep connection of brotherhood in his experience with Robert that he felt was often missing in the play between men in the larger world.

The gifts for everyone in the room poured out.

Bernadette's guilt and regret vanished in a way that seemed magical, but was really a profoundly simple demonstration of how the past can be shifted in the present with openness, curiosity, and trust. Bernadette didn't have to let go of anything or try to find something else. She simply came into appreciation of the love that had been waiting for more than a quarter-century to be seen.

Chapter 5
Blow It Out of Proportion

"When the music changes, so does the dance."

~ Hausa proverb

"I knew as soon as it came out of my mouth, it was the *wrong* thing to say," Sue relayed during our phone session, recounting a recent conversation with a guy she'd been on-again off-again dating for some time. "I actually began to shake while I was talking to him. I was pacing around my apartment. My response was uncontrollable. I sort of knew it was happening as it was happening, but I couldn't control it. It was as if I was lobbing a grenade to blow something up, on purpose."

"At the very least, I blew things *way* out of proportion," Sue admitted, after taking a pause for a breath. Her shame was clearly palpable.

She filled in the details of the story, another version of one she lived out in many ways. This time, the war zone was her social life.

"He told me I was making it all about me, and I was. I guess I wasn't listening to him the way he wanted me to.

29

I do have this pattern of either making it all about other people or all about myself. But I realized it and apologized. It's hard to know if he really heard me. But I haven't been able to shake the feeling it was a major screw-up. At the same time, I look at myself and realize it wasn't that big a deal. Whatever I said to him was really a small thing. It's like I love self-punishment or something …"

I let Sue talk. I was listening for the clues she'd unknowingly leave behind in the words she spoke, like a Hansel and Gretel trail of pebbles or breadcrumbs that would lead through obstacles to an eventual safe haven. But as many stories of perceived challenge do, Sue's quickly turned to her childhood. It's a familiar place we all revisit when searching for the source of something gone wrong.

She began to cite examples of how her parents often treated her badly, making them responsible for the behaviors she hated in herself today. One after another, more grenades were lobbed. These she tossed at her parents, aiming the explosives at long ago, fuses lit with blame. It's a combat tactic we all know well.

"For example," Sue said, "one time I didn't load my clothes from the washer into the dryer before leaving the house for school. Do you believe my mother actually *called* the school and had the office announce my name over the loudspeaker with the message that I needed to come home and finish my laundry?" She didn't wait for my reply before going on. "And this was when I was in *high school*, not grade school. I was absolutely humiliated. It was always stuff like that. The punishments were always way out of proportion to my supposed crimes."

"Sounds to me like you're serving a life sentence," I said with a chuckle.

Sue had been a student in two programs I taught, so she was familiar with how I worked. She knew I wouldn't offer much in the way of sympathy to ease her wounded soul. I was more committed to helping her locate the wisdom in the presenting unpleasant circumstance than I was to helping her feel better. It was the war-in-the-name-of-love tactic I used before lobbing my own grenades at the harsh judgments that were calling the shots in most aspects of her life.

After Sue further indicted her parents to substantiate her penchant for self-punishment, I could hear the locked pattern call up from the tomb of her past. *Exhume me, please*, it pleaded. I was gearing up for the moment in the movie where I could play the part of Toto, gripping the bottom of the curtain and pulling it back with my teeth to expose the powerful wizard at the controls. Except in this case, it wouldn't be a wounded and eccentric imposter in hiding. It would be Sue's special miracle-making wizardry that was revealed.

It's always easier to flow with the course of the river than try to change its direction.

One of the things I knew about Sue was that she was a devoted practitioner and teacher of homeopathy, a healing remedy that created out-of-proportion outcomes for others from tiny inputs.

Her wizardry also manifested another way. Music was a huge part of Sue's life as well. In one of the classes she attended, she became known as the "DJ shaman"; she was always cuing up the perfectly themed lyric and song to play during a class break or as a shake-it-out dance number. Sue often posted photos of concerts on Facebook, forever managing to get backstage passes or seats to sold-out shows. She had the greatest ticket karma of anyone I knew.

"Sue, let's shift perspective for a minute." I paused, assembling a small bomb of a question that would link the value of the pattern she carried to the expression she was beating up with judgment. "Don't you get ridiculously big results with very little effort when it comes to music? For a moment, can you try taking that on as made of the same stuff as this story of big punishments for small crimes?"

The question was barely out of my mouth before Sue started giggling on the other end of the phone.

My grenade exploded and it turned into a gorgeous fireworks display.

"Oh, it's *way* more than that," she replied, before launching into a short monologue. Her voice had more power now. She was also having much more fun with this than listing the numerous offenses of her harshly punitive parents.

"When I went to school at NYU, I walked right into the stuff of my dreams. I landed an internship at Columbia Records within the first year of living in New York. Crazy shit happened all the time. One day, David Gilmour from Pink Floyd popped his head inside my office door to chat while I was working at my desk. And then there was the time that Paul McCartney was brought through each of the departments at Columbia to meet the work teams. They were staging a group photograph while I watched from the corner. After the photographer took the shot, Paul looked at me, asked who I was, and motioned me over to him. He put his arm around me and then had his guy take a photo of just the two of us. I was the only person in the whole building who got their picture taken alone with Sir Paul that day." It was easy to tell from the sound of her voice that it was a milestone moment.

"So listen to what you're saying," I interrupted, despite being curious to hear more of her adventures. "Do you get that this is the same energy you've been complaining about? It's another way things blow out of proportion for you. You're in the corner doing nothing but watching, and suddenly Paul McCartney has his arm around you—a big return from little effort.

"It's all where you choose to focus, Sue. Look at where it plays out in your life. It's embedded in your work as a homeopath. It's the gist of your great music karma. And it's tied up with your forty-year resentment about big punishments for small crimes with your mom … never mind condemning yourself for blowing things out of proportion in the call with what's-his-name. It's all in how you hold it. It's a lot faster to make the big and dramatic work for you than to focus on being a victim of it.

"Sue, the awareness you feed today creates the reality you'll encounter tomorrow. Why not try owning your wizardry in being able to make big things happen from small shifts in consciousness?"

After my own monologue was complete, I asked, "Do you know who you have to thank for that mastery?"

Without waiting for her reply, I answered the question myself.

"Your parents, love. Maybe cut them a break? If you're going to make them responsible by way of blame, can you also give them a few deserved awards? Maybe a Grammy or two?" I chuckled, half-serious.

Her laugh echoed through the phone. "You're right. It always does come down to appreciation. You know, the other day I tried to get seats for a show next month. I didn't look at the dates before going online to buy the tickets.

And I got locked out before the venue sold out. That almost never happens to me. Not five minutes later, a friend called to say she'd gotten us seats for the same show. Except in the meantime, I realized I had to be out of town that weekend. I was pissed when I realized I still had to miss it after all. I knew it was a ridiculous response, given how much great music I've seen in my life. So I decided to make an alphabetical list, starting at the letter A and ending at Z, of twenty-six shows I've been lucky enough to go to. I know it's about being grateful …" her voice trailed off before finishing. "And I got stuck at twenty-five—until I remembered Zappa." Sue was almost giddy now.

"Well, that makes your homework easy." I handed down her orders from my military command post on the other end of the phone. Instead of drop-and-give-me-ten, I said, "A to Z. I want you to do the work of remembering all the ways your parents did well by you. One for each of the twenty-six letters of the alphabet, to follow the map your story gave me. Create a ritual or ceremony that deepens the gratitude practice." I knew she knew how to do that from our classroom work together.

"And Sue?" I added. "Maybe it's time for you to accept this pattern of making really big consequences out of little or no action and put it to work in your life. Get ready for it to play out in a larger context and watch for the evidence."

I finished by guiding her through an experience to ground what had unfolded in our conversation. I led her to use her breath to circulate this re-purposed pattern in an experiential voyage through her central nervous system. Together, we rode inhales and exhales, glided along neural pathways and leaped over synapses, literally using her breath to blow on the sparks of awareness of the beauty of this pattern, so it would ignite. We used the well-worn neural paths to re-pave trails of robust possibility, rather than engage a loop of former disasters. We did this until she was "wearing" the pattern imaginatively and somatically, fully engaged in her senses.

When we were complete, there was a deep silence on the phone lines between us. I sensed her inward journey was also an expedition into the heavenly realms where there were no degrees of separation between Sue and other stars. If she used her will to get behind the unfolding of her life from this perspective, anything would be possible. Like all of the small stories we tell, it was never about her boyfriend, or even her parents. It was about something much, much bigger, something so big and out of proportion that Sue's own greatness could become her new life sentence.

Chapter 6
Practice Beginner's Mind

"Daniel, would you like to have your dad stay and hang with us? Or should he stay out in the waiting room?" I asked the ten-year-old boy whose father looked on in anticipation while standing in the doorway of my office.

"No, that's okay, I'm good," Daniel responded, gently dismissing his dad.

Daniel's father, Russell, was a single parent, martial artist, salsa dancer, and highly successful computer programmer. He was one of my clients and had taken a program I taught a couple of years earlier. His son was equally talented, the proverbial apple having clearly fallen not so far from the tree. Russell jokingly referred to him as "Mini-Me."

As he sat deep in the angled seat in front of me, Daniel's arms relaxed against the curved wooden armrests. He looked small in the big chair, which was usually occupied by adults three or more times his age and weight. Still, he filled up the space with a humble, wise presence.

Children naturally hold what Buddhists refer to as "beginner's mind": the ability to remain receptive and impressionable. Often the keepers of overlooked wisdom, kids have a simple ability to cut to the core of things, at least until consensual reality conditions them to filter their experience. Daniel and I got to know each other for a bit before circling to the purpose of his visit.

"So, Daniel, when your dad called, he told me a little bit about what's going on for you. But I'd really like to hear from you what's been happening at school lately."

"I'm being bullied," Daniel replied with a note of directness in his voice, picking a word he probably heard often. He went on to tell me the story about the boy who was giving him a hard time and the involvement of his dad and teacher in the matter. I listened intently to him before I shifted the subject.

"Hey, are you a fan of super-heroes, Daniel?"

He named several famous comic-book and movie characters and a few I didn't know, probably from the world of video games.

As he did this, I lifted three large stones from the urn of rocks that sat on the floor next to Daniel's chair and laid them out in the shape of a triangle. I was recreating a three-dimensional representation of a social model offered to me many years earlier, during my training. It's referred to as the Drama Triangle, a trinity of the persecutor, the victim, and the rescuer, which is said to organize around incidents of trauma, regardless of whether they're big or small. Originally envisioned by Dr. Stephen Karpman with roots in his study of Transactional Analysis, the Drama Triangle was adapted by my teacher to illustrate how each of the three roles disempowers all the participants involved.

"So let's imagine this big stone represents a bully, kinda like the kid at school," I said, pointing to the rock on the lower left, facing him. "And maybe this smaller one over here can be the bully's target, kinda like you." Then I pointed at the stone straight across. "And this one at the top can be one of those super-heroes, the one above and between the two, ready to fly in for the rescue."

Daniel watched carefully.

For me, the three points of the triangle hit the plot lines of nearly every story of challenge and difficulty we experience and retell, whether we were ten or a hundred and ten. When I was first introduced to the triangle as a student, it was presented as a way to mark where we could become caught in a disempowering relationship. The triangle was also the place, over time, where victims later became persecutors who either perpetuated patterns of harm or morphed into rescuers desperately trying to stop the madness they were once a part of. As a young student, I was unable to find the angles that connected bully, victim, and rescuer as useable in some way, so focusing on stepping out of disempowerment seemed sensible.

But over time, I became curious about stepping in differently rather than only stepping out. It seemed to me that steps went both ways. I realized that if I stepped out of or away from something I was trying to avoid, that very thing would follow my footsteps and track me down somewhere else. So I became curious about stepping into the triangle in a different way. I needed to find something trustworthy deep in the essence of victim, rescuer, and persecutor.

Daniel was about to help me do just that.

"What do bullies really do, Daniel?"

"They start trouble," he replied immediately.

"So in order to be a really *bad* bully, you have to be a really *good* starter?" I probed, knowing he probably hadn't considered the essential, neutral quality of a bully before. Neither did most adults I knew.

"Well, I *guess* that's true," he replied, reluctantly, and with a quizzical look on his face.

I watched the wheels turn in his head. I had seen the same expression from his dad many times before.

"Do you mean that I should think of a bully as a good starter?" Daniel was clearly gifted well beyond his years in simple logic.

"Well, not so much that you *should* think or do any-thing … It's kinda just something to notice. Because maybe if a bully is a good starter, he could also be good at starting something other than trouble. But I think it may be pretty hard to see that when you feel like the target of a bully. That kinda sucks, doesn't it?" I was thinking I might be way over Daniel's ten-year-old head with this. But I underestimated how bright he was.

I watched as his gaze slowly trailed to the smaller stone across from the bully rock. I sensed we couldn't look at the bully's target quite yet. It was too close for Daniel's comfort. He needed a little more distance. Then as the trail of his eyes moved to the stone at the top, I watched him follow the path of my thoughts.

"Well, what about that stone?" he asked, pointing to the one at the high point of the triangle. "The rescuing superhero one?"

"You tell me," I replied. "If a bully can be a good starter, what does a superhero do?" I totally expected Daniel to tell me that he comes in to save the day.

"Well, Dad and my teacher are like rescuers," he said precociously, pausing before adding, "and I hate it."

Daniel's statement surprised me. I expected him to feel relieved by the intervention of his father and teacher in the situation at school, not to be so resentful of it. But that was my story, not his.

"Well, rescuers are kinda like superheroes, aren't they? And who doesn't like a superhero? You just named a few of your favorites a little while ago, remember? If you don't like them rescuing you, what if they had another perfect mission?"

Daniel sat quietly for a little bit; the computer behind his eyes hummed before he delivered his sage answer. "Yeah, I guess rescuers *are* like superheroes. But a superhero's real job should be to teach other people to be their own superheroes."

I was stunned. Ten years old. For a long time, I'd played with lots of different ideas about the value of being a rescuer—and Daniel nailed it after thinking about it for sixty seconds. He'd fully repurposed the rescuer for me in one sentence. Daniel also articulated a fuller paradigm about personal and professional helpers.

I'd been on that particular path for some time. I'd even once joked with my best friend, a divinity-school grad and highly successful professional coach, how we might one day answer our office phones with a short hello, followed by, "And how can I *not* help you?"

Somehow hearing this from Daniel allowed me to integrate the strong pull I had toward teaching, knowing at the same time I had nothing, really, to offer others, other than a more loving connection with themselves.

While I may have gained far more wow than Daniel did in our short meeting, something super-powerful created the space for him to speak up to his dad and teacher about not wanting to be rescued, even if meant he'd be enduring a little emotional bruising on the playground.

Sometimes a little target practice, or practice as the target, can teach a hero a super-powerful lesson.

Chapter 7

Love De-Man-d

"I blame my father, really," Tebbe said in reply to my question about why he hadn't yet brought himself to make a full-time living as an artist. We were on a hunt together to find the source of that story.

A recent Facebook post he put up spoke to it all:

"Support living artists. The dead ones don't need it."

Tebbe had just finished telling me his version of the story of his dad, a gifted photographer who placed a passion for his art aside in order to earn a Ph.D. He then worked hard to support his family as a chemical engineer. As Tebbe grew up, he saw himself as the shadow of his father, with similar talent and gifts, but stalled by his father's continual redirection of Tebbe away from engaging in art as anything but a hobby.

This was the perfect example of how stories and experiences get passed down from generation to generation.

Because he was busy blaming his father, Tebbe couldn't harness his own ability to provide strong financial support for his family. Without a loving connection to the dad who was a great provider, he couldn't see himself at all like his father or become fully expressed as a provider himself. Tebbe was unable to see the successful and financially secure chemical engineer living within him, the engineer of absolute beauty. He used chemicals of a different kind—the paints he mixed on his palette.

As he told the story about his father, it all came down to a single robust memory.

"The one thing I'll never forget was the day he *demanded* I either find a job or get out of the house. I remember him slamming his fist down on the kitchen table. I was beyond pissed. I was bitter. And I left, all right," his voice carrying the angry bite of a threatening recollection. "I went as far in the opposite direction as I could possibly go. For a *very* long time."

The memory was well-etched in Tebbe, imaginably in the same way an illustration of beauty lived within him before being carried to the canvas for expression. Except this memory was expressed on the living canvas of a challenged financial life.

"You know what I hear in this, Teb?" I asked. "The word that stands out is demand. De-man, your dad, demanded you go out, make your own way, and earn a living."

It was so very clear to me that "demand" held the key to his story. It wasn't to be avoided; it was to be taken on in an even bigger way.

"Listen," I offered, "what if you unwound all the denunciation of your father and all the judgment you carry about the word 'demand'? What if *you* became de-man? What if you used your dad's voice as your voice to direct yourself in answering the call to create a market demand for your amazing artwork?"

There was a pause on the end of the phone. As we all do in similar kinds of circumstances when something has been carried forever as an experience of victimization, Tebbe pushed back.

"Wait a minute. My father didn't believe I could make it in the art world. He wanted to me to do what he did, to conform to his expectations or get out of the house. There wasn't anything good about that."

Picturing him in front of me, I imagined Tebbe to be physically digging his heels in, rather than tapping them together three times to go back to a different version of the story of his family home.

"Tell me, Teb," I asked, "what's the difference between an invitation and a demand?" There was another long pause on the line. I could tell he was sinking into the question.

"Well, with an invitation, you have a choice of whether or not you want to respond. With a demand, it's still a request, but it feels like there's little choice in the matter. It's insistent—the I-won't-take-no-for-an-answer kinda thing."

"Exactly," I replied. "The source of energy is the same. It points to the same thing. It can be offered in hand-printed calligraphy as a polite and formal invitation or it can be a raw ultimatum. Listen, what does it really matter? Who cares if your father wasn't aware that he was giving you a tremendous gift? When we're asleep, it sometimes takes demand to get our attention." My voice dropped into quiet through the phone lines. "If we unwrap the judgment, we get to work with what's there with love and as wisdom." After a pause, I added, "For what it's worth, I bet this was a loving request all along. Trust me, Teb, it's a lot faster to take it in, accept it, and convert it in a way you want to use it than to try like hell to keep fighting that current in the river as if you can change the way it pushes against you. You've been doing it that way for more than forty years."

In the stillness on the other end of the phone, I could *hear* Tebbe thinking deeply.

I continued, "What if your dad gifted you the one thing you needed to make it for yourself? To demand that you step up and accept the raw invitation of making your way in the world as an artist—doing what you love—with absolutely no room to decline? What if by rejecting him, you also rejected the provider, the success of the chemical engineer? And the demand that made *him* step out of his house to meet the world that was waiting for him?"

Tebbe was crying softly on the other end of the phone. "Well, yes, that feels right. Of course, I never thought about it that way before. I never imagined my father as anything but non-supportive of my being an artist. I spent years pissed off at him, and struggling …" His voice trailed off.

At the end of our call, I suggested Tebbe do some work to honor his dad, to lift him up, so the father, the provider energy, could lift him up in turn. He needed to bring this other way of telling the story of his father into an experience. Tebbe was well-practiced at creating ways of honoring, of using ceremony to take it into an experience and not just remain an idea. His tools of ritual were paintbrushes and canvas. In this case, it didn't matter what kind of honoring he did, as long as he elevated the memory of his father to another level. He needed to accept his dad's demand as the request of a God-father that could not be refused.

With painting as his ceremony, financially profitable creative engineering could become his experience.

Some months later, after Tebbe began producing and selling paintings at nearly twice the rate of the same period in the prior year, we spoke again.

"Did you see what I posted on Facebook last week?" he asked when we first got on the phone.

I knew what he was referring to: A few days before, he put a striking painting of an Asheville, North Carolina, alleyway on his timeline. The colors were rich. The serpentine walkway in the foreground was puddled with rain and wove its way in a curve under a cloudy sky at nightfall. The pooled water on the ground reflected the light emanating from the windows of buildings that lined the alley's edge.

"I got a ton of comments," he said. "Over seventy-five, I think." Tebbe was beginning to engage the world by answering his father's demand and naturally creating a market *demand* for his work.

"I saw that," I answered. "It was a brilliant piece. The colors were incredible. But what struck me the most was the invitation to your friends to suggest titles for it. Didn't you offer something to the person whose title you picked?"

"I did," Tebbe replied. "I offered the winner a full rendering of the painting in exchange. I couldn't believe so many people took the time to respond."

It didn't surprise me at all. Tebbe was beginning to step into his father's demand. He was *getting out of the house,* all right. A little differently than his father demanded that he do at eighteen, but his work was getting out. He was beginning to wear the idea of demand in a new way. He was making tangible progress in bringing his artwork to the world.

"I love that you invited everyone to help you name the painting," I said to Tebbe.

Not until after it came out of my mouth did I hear it. It was in the word "name." In my listening, it had a slight echo. It would have been easy to overlook. But I train myself to pay attention to echoes, visual traces I see in my mind's eye, and gut feelings that rise up, as I come in contact with peoples' stories.

Once again, it was hidden in plain sight. When I first met Tebbe, his name was Kevin. Then he switched to Tebbe, his middle name.

"Hey, I've got a question for you, and I think it's a connection to today's work," I said, eager to hear his reply. "When exactly did you change your name from Kevin to Tebbe?"

"It was when we moved to Asheville," he answered. "One of the reasons we chose Asheville was because it had such an incredible art community. I really wanted a memorable name as an artist to associate with my work. So I dropped Kevin and decided to go by Tebbe. It's definitely more of an artist's name."

I could also *feel* the fact that the name Kevin was deeply related to the teenager who was thrown out of his father's house. Kevin, placed aside, held the part of him that wasn't successful, that was still bitter. I could feel something swelling to the surface. We were about to bring another piece of his story back home.

"Okay," I said. "Let's play a little game. You know it well; hell, you invented it. Take out a pencil and paper and create a quick sketch. We're going to re-enact the Facebook naming contest."

Only three seconds passed before Tebbe piped up at the other end of the phone. "Done," he announced lightly.

"Okay," I replied. "Take a picture of what you sketched and text it to me."

This is what arrived:

"Now, my friend, name the sketch. I'll give you a full rendering in return if I use it in my book," I laughed, borrowing from his own pitch to his Facebook followers.

When he answered, the ether between Connecticut and North Carolina suddenly went from playful to serious.

"*Kevin Takes a Beating,*" Tebbe offered, in stone-cold reply. Quickly after he spoke, he added with a discouraged-sounding sigh, "It's never over."

I wasn't certain if he was offering a second idea for a title for the sketch or just a statement of recognition about the well-worn neural highway that led him, again and again, to feel like the victim in a struggle with his father.

"Okay, my turn. Here's what I'd call the image, based on what I see. Are you ready?" Then I said, "*The Zen Monk.*"

When I saw Tebbe's drawing, it instantly conjured a monk carrying a Japanese *kyosaku* stick, otherwise known as the "warning" or "awakening" stick. It's wielded by the *jikijitsu*, the head monk who is put in charge of the sleepy meditators in the *zendo* or meditation hall. In Soto Zen, the *kyosaku* stick is always "administered" *at the request* of the meditator, by way of bowing one's head, putting the palms together in a prayerful position, then exposing each shoulder to be struck in turn.

Tebbe's sketch had all the elements. The meditator was asking for awakening from the *jikijitsu*, using the blow to shatter his sleepiness.

Certainly, nothing having to do with a victim appeared in this way of telling the story.

"Teb, we've talked about your dad before and a lot has shifted since the first time we did. But we haven't really talked about Kevin. You renamed yourself—and the title you chose for this little picture tells us the story you still carry about Kevin."

Tebbe was quiet for about a minute on the other end of the line before he replied. "Wow. Wow! It's all right here. You're right. I can focus on the story I've carried around all these years about Kevin getting beaten down or I can see this as part of the awakening process. There it is again. My dad offered me an opportunity to awaken."

I could hear the tears flooding the state of North Carolina.

"Perhaps," I said quietly, "but if we look at this picture in the way of the Soto Zen monk, all the power, and the request to be struck, come *from the meditator*, the one who seeks the awakening. Listen, it's great to give dad the long-awaited credit he deserves, but this one is on you, my friend."

The sigh Tebbe released as he listened on the other end was a low whistle. "You mean I've created this?" he half-asked and half-stated.

No reply was my reply.

After a minute or two, we went on to talk about Kevin and how he dropped the name, as well as a part of himself, in the same way he condemned and distanced his dad with his judgment. Tebbe had avoided Kevin, rather than joining the artist and the son-turned-provider together.

Without Kevin, Tebbe couldn't fully make a living selling his art. Kevin's destiny was to be a provider like his dad. Instead, he was recreating the archetypal story of the starving artist who couldn't feed his family. The two needed to merge, bound together by love and connection, rather than judgment and separation.

"It's the perfect trifecta," Tebbe said, out of nowhere.

"What do you mean?"

"My name," he replied. "I need to bring Kevin back in. I still want to go by Tebbe as my first name, but I can switch the two and be Tebbe *Kevin* Davis. You know, I've kept my name legally, because I felt I owed it to my mother. But I'm taking it back where it can be supported between Tebbe-the-artist and my father's name, Davis. Kevin needs to go in the middle."

I felt tears well up in my eyes as I said, "Yup. Kevin is finally giving himself the support he needs to succeed, with Mom and Dad on either side."

It doesn't matter how old we are when we get it, because it's ultimately not even our own mothers and fathers we're talking about. I suddenly understood why in indigenous cultures there was a rite of passage for those in adolescence to be released by their biological parents and connected instead to Mother Earth and Father Sky.

Then, I had to say, "Hey Teb? Thanks."

Though he couldn't see it through the phone lines, I bowed my head. It was an acknowledgment of our mutual willingness to remain open to even deeper levels of awakening.

Chapter 8

Roll with the Stones

"So who feels called to volunteer?"

My gaze panned the group of twenty in front of me. I was teaching for the organization where, as a student, I trained in the fundamentals of shifting perceptual states, a skill attributed to shamans across many cultures. In my periphery, someone leaned far forward to catch my eye.

Jackie was a powerhouse of a woman. In addition to being the mother of two young boys, she held a doctorate in nutrition and carried a tremendous passion for educating kids on how to eat and parents and schools on how to raise healthy children by feeding them well. She was a new client in my practice, so though I didn't know her well, I was aware of her fears and dreams. I'd invited her to the group, confident it would deepen the insights I offered her in our private sessions.

Jackie had talked to me about wanting another child and hoped for a girl, but strains in her marriage held her back from getting pregnant. She was also a breast-cancer survivor, having undergone a partial mastectomy about a year before we met. Not much kept her down. She was super bright, articulate, and absolutely full of life.

Early on in the class, which was about practices derived from the medicine and wisdom of South American indigenous culture, she recognized that her draw to participate was more about using the tools offered as a springboard for making a fuller claim on who she already was. Jackie wasn't much interested in working with sacred stones or power animals as she was in being a *food shaman*—a half-playful half-serious tagline that followed her through the remainder of our meetings.

When Jackie arrived for the weekend, she took me aside near the doorway of our classroom. "I'm trying to keep my anxieties about this in check, Pat, but I found a small lump in my other breast. I'm going in for an ultrasound next week. I just wanted to let you know what was going on."

Though we didn't have a chance to speak directly about it again during the course of the weekend, I kept a watch on her. She appeared more settled toward the end of the class than she did when she arrived on Friday. As the time neared to head home, I sensed her concern resurface. It was visible as she leaned in to respond to my request for a volunteer. When our eyes met, I waved her up to take a seat in the chair next to me.

"Okay, Jackie, I'd like you to pick out something that calls to you from here," pointing down to a group of stones arranged on a colorful cloth at my feet. After she bent over to select one and pulled herself upright again, I slowed the cadence of my words and dropped the tone of my voice to a soft hush.

"If you would, Jackie, close your eyes and go inside. Take a few breaths and sense where you are, right now, as you are, after all of your work this weekend. When you're ready—and take your time—I want you to blow the essence of who you are and how you are right now into the stone you picked."

After several long exhalations, Jackie opened her eyes and handed the stone back to me.

"I'm going to demonstrate a simple but foundational practice that we'll build on from here on out." I turned away from Jackie to address the group using the instructional tone of teacher-voice. I wanted to emphasize the power of the simple. I knew from my own training and practice that if students gave themselves fully to the exercise, over time it would expand their capacity to see and hear across a broader spectrum.

"Using the gateways of each of my five senses, I'll *read* this stone to get a little more data about what's present and unfolding in Jackie. I'm *not* reading her future; I'm exploring her *now*."

I paused before going on. "For those of you who think you haven't yet developed a capacity to do this, think of it this way. We all share a common field of human experience. It may be easier for you to frame this as being aware of what's available in the present moment in *you*. So when the time comes for you to sit and hold the stone your partner blew into, you can take that road. It will bring you to the same place."

And that was what happened. With Jackie's chair parked next to mine, I sensed that her mind was beginning to wonder what lay ahead of her back home and in the doctor's office the next week. In the land beyond her and me, it didn't matter who was generating the impressions that arose. They were simply in plain sight.

There is no possession of what is co-created in the space of shared experience.

Holding the stone she gave me, I closed my eyes to break from the role of demonstrator to one of experiencer, then re-opened them and looked down at what lay in the palm of my hand, engaging my sense of sight.

What I saw surprised me, it was so vivid and immediate. Like Jackie's persona, it was quick and forthcoming. It didn't mess around. Following suit, I held the stone up and reported what had appeared to me.

"Well, uh … wow, that was fast. Normally, I probably would've turned the stone this way and that, taken in its color and line and contour, and spoke about it in pretty general stone-like terms, even as I was reading Jackie. But it sort of shape-shifted in front of me.

"Do you see the split here?" I pointed to the deep groove in the rock when I turned it to a sideways position. "Well, I saw this as the ridge of an upper lip and the one below it as the lower. Then I saw a huge tongue hanging out, exactly like the logo on a Rolling Stones album cover."

I refrained from mentioning to the group that as much as I wanted to be true to what I saw, I was already hoping what I encountered next when reading for Jackie would be a little less inane, so I didn't have a room full of people looking for legendary rock stars in their own set of stones a few minutes later! Seriously, we mostly learn by imitation before locking in the knowledge through personal experience.

A few heads were nodding, either in polite respect, or in receptivity to my suggestion, or because with the addition of a little imagination, they could see the pair of oversized lips for themselves—or even because they were remembering all the great songs on *Sticky Fingers*, the first album to display the iconic Rolling Stones logo.

Then I lifted the stone to my ear. The response here was equally unsubtle and, unfortunately, much worse if my inner judge was any indication. I'd apparently bumped into a theme, or encountered the very trend I feared only seconds before. I heard Mick Jagger singing out this line from the famous song: "You can't always get what you want … but if you try sometime … you just might find … you get what you need." It amplified its way out of the crack in the stone as if a tiny microphone were embedded within.

Ordinarily, a few seconds would tick by in emptiness before continuing my report to Jackie and the group. Instead, movement froze in the room and time stretched far apart to make way for a tsunami of thoughts to stream through, riding a wave of milliseconds. My brain felt like it was doing what Charlton Heston/Moses did for the Jews when parting the Red Sea in *The Ten Commandments*.

What if Jackie interprets what I say as she can't get what she wants—a clean bill of health?

What if her cancer isn't in full and permanent remission?

What if I'm about to plant a seed of negativity as she's leaving this weekend, when she looks so much more at peace then she did when she arrived?

What if I get this wrong? I want to get this right and right must mean that Jackie gets what she wants.

Isn't that what we're here on Earth for? To create the life we want? To pretend we're in full control and power over everything in our lives?

Imposter!

Or worse, what if you're creating a self-fulfilling prophecy? That seed of concern might be enough to tank her immune response and make her sick again.

The mental onslaught withdrew as I removed the stone from my ear. I looked down at it, to see Mick's lips morph into Kali, the Hindu Dark Goddess of Destruction and Creation, sticking out her blue-black tongue at me, offering,

I supposed, her opinion on the voice of resistance. Then the parted Red Sea folded back, swallowing the last remaining thoughts that made it out of the gate before they reached my full awareness. The room began to move again—and I simply spoke.

I stayed true to what was present, shared with Jackie and the rest of the room what I heard, and went about the rest of my demonstration. Shortly after, the students had their own practice of the exercise. The weekend was complete. All was well.

One thing I learned very early on, despite bouts of challenge and occasional total forgetting, was to trust, even when subject to the interrogation of an army of charging internal naysayers.

The wisdom that took longer for me to acquire, through direct experience rather than being told so by someone else, was never to assume that trust always lines up with desire. The offerings of the holy are often the opposite of what we want. They don't sort for our willingness to receive them. They're abundantly bestowed, like them or not.

About ten days later, Jackie called me.

"Pat, I just wanted to let you know the ultrasound was clear. I'm so relieved. But you know what's funny? While I was in the waiting room to get the test results, you'll *never* guess what song played over the sound system ..."

I *heard* her big smile on the other end of the phone and of course, I didn't have to guess; we both knew I knew already. Jackie got what she needed, because it was exactly what happened.

What we need is never apart from what happens.

Part 2

Awakening and Unfolding Magic

Chapter 9

Don't Leap to Conclusions

A house leaves you as you leave it
all the memories carrying their suitcases
with the moments packed inside

that leave in dreams
walking single file
out the door behind your eyes

a house leaves in stages
the way it was built

a house lets you go
a piece at a time
clearing out its drawers
mopping up the floors

emptying the closets
where the things that kept you warm
once lived...

tugging at your sleeve to stay
guiding you to the door
where tomorrow stands in the street

waiting

~Robert Cole, excerpted from "A House Leaves in Dreams"

ೞ

Kevin and Lisa, sans astronaut gear, sat spinning across from each other in the orbit of my office beneath a NASA photo of stars and planets that hung on the wall.

"I think we should go live in Bali while we still can. I want to ride to the village market to buy warm bread and carry it back home in the front basket of my bike. Lily could sleep in a sling as I peddle," Lisa joked, half-sarcastic, but with a hint of absolute seriousness.

Right after her comment, Kevin turned to me to add, "If we don't make a break for it now, we may never go. We have no house to sell; the kids are young enough, so we don't have to pull them out of school. We can make this happen. *Now* is the time." Kevin was sitting on the plum La-Z-Boy chair to my right. He had a slight tan, evidence of his recent trip to Haiti and out of place in the early New England spring. It was the first time he'd been away since their son was born three years earlier. Little Shawn really missed him during the ten-day excursion, as did Lisa, who was still adjusting to a part-time return to her business, while continuing to nurse their six-month-old daughter Lily.

I spoke with Lisa during the time Kevin was away. She jokingly likened the experience of his absence to the movie *The Martian*, the story of an astronaut left behind on the desolate red planet as his fellow travelers rocketed toward home, having assumed him for dead. In the ten days Kevin was gone, she, like the main character in the film, had to confront her own version of a survival story. For her, this meant balancing being back to work and meeting the needs of their two young children all on her own.

Lisa immediately dismissed what Kevin said, jumping in as devil's advocate. "Easy for you to say. You just got back from Haiti and still have the afterglow. Believe me, you'll miss your six-dollar Starbucks coffee." This was the same woman who, moments ago, was happily peddling to and from the Balinese village market.

Mars and Earth appeared miles apart.

After their second child was born, Kevin and Lisa, both spirited adventurists, finally made a decision. During Lisa's pregnancy, they'd toyed with the idea of moving out of state, but gave in to circumstance and put roots down locally.

For the past couple of years, they'd been housesitting for a family living in Europe. With no set end to their arrangement, they approached the owners to see if they were interested in selling the house to them. The answer was yes; the homeowners were putting down their own roots in the UK. So Lisa and Kevin happily "pinky swore" to each other that they would lay the topic of moving to rest and let go of thinking they would find greater happiness and a more like-minded community anywhere other than where they were ... at least for a time.

It turned out to be a very short time.

Just a few weeks into formalizing the plans for purchase, a serious and unanticipated medical diagnosis arose for one of the homeowners, who now needed to return from abroad and reclaim their Connecticut residence to be closer to a familiar medical system and extended family. For Lisa and Kevin, the engagement with settling in proved to be nothing more than brief flirtation.

Though they came to my office to explore the idea of what to do next, they already held an absolute mastery from which to draw.

Lisa was a skilled massage therapist who taught anatomy to yoga teachers on a national level. She had an appreciation of mechanics and structure and knew intuitively how to build both bodies and balanced ideas from the ground up and the inside out. Kevin's business periodically took him across the globe to various developing countries. He supervised teams of volunteers who constructed simple homes for those who lived in abject poverty, many times in resource-scarce areas where what little infrastructure was there to begin with had been toppled by an event like an earthquake or tsunami.

While by comparison a far gentler circumstance for Lisa and Kevin, this was the metaphorical equivalent of a temblor. The tectonic plates of the desired and the unexpected had collided and the question of where they would call home rose from the rubble. This time they weren't grappling with whether they'd initiate a change. Fate forced it.

Kevin had a tired, pensive look on his face. Of the two, he seemed more poised and ready to make a break for it, to not only revisit the tabled conversation, but to raise the stakes from an out-of-state to an out-of-country move.

Lisa's recent experience of the isolation of *The Martian* was clearly still hovering around her, in conflict with her attraction to idyllic living in a warm and sunny place far away. Would the seductive story of better weather turn into living in a tropical paradise? Or would such weather prove as hot, isolating, and foreign as a trip to the red planet?

It was clear that both of them had been going back and forth with the pros and cons in the days since receiving the call from Europe. They were agonizing over not only what was best for them, but also for their young children, involved grandparents, and their two businesses.

When they arrived at my office, they weren't so much stressed as caught *in-decision* and toying with the idea of making a big leap to the far end of their dreams.

Having seen *The Martian* myself, I sat listening to them and recalled the scene where Matt Damon, playing the brilliant astronaut abandoned on Mars, seeded the freeze-dried potato side-dish packets from the ship's galley into the crew's left-behind excrement. Out of the unpleasant, he grew a crop that ultimately sustained him while he sought to define home in a very unexpected circumstance.

Kevin and Lisa came to me so that I could remind them to trust that everything they needed was already in and around them, even though sometimes things weren't crystal clear.

In fact, creative opportunities almost always revealed themselves out of the dark, like the astronaut's unappealing, but lifesaving, compost.

"Since this already feels like an impossible choice, why don't we just trust that?" I offered. "Don't make a decision."

They both turned to me simultaneously with the look I sometimes get when I suggest embracing what's happening as it's happening, rather than trying to make something else happen. They stared at me from their two points of orbit at my suggestion of calling off the search for a conclusion.

"How about letting home choose you? Even better," I added, "what if you trust that it already has?"

Chapter 10

Dim the Lights

"She was pure light," Sandy told me, her voice cracking through the phone when she called to make an appointment to see me.

Her mentor, a highly successful forty-something woman with children the same age as Sandy's, had passed away just a few weeks earlier, losing her fight with breast cancer.

"I feel like I owe it to her to shine as brightly as I can. She did so much for me. I don't know that I can ever beam quite like she did. But I feel it's the next level that's calling. I want to become a world-class coach and teacher, and hold that in balance with being a good partner and parent. I owe it to her and myself to do that work. I'm really, really hungry for it."

Before her arrival, I made a point of setting out a number of tea lights in small globes around the room, creating a trail of light that stretched back to the words she spoke in our initial call. And sure enough, when she arrived at my office a week later, a supernova burst through the door. A bright and dynamic woman, Sandy was an executive coach and trainer working for a major international corporation.

"I know I'm a great coach." Sandy settled into the leather loveseat. "That's ninety percent of what I do. But what I love to do is to teach." She said she felt most energized when working with groups. "When I walk in to facilitate a training with other leaders, I'm always the brightest bulb in the room." Her voice dropped slightly to humble her honest admission. "But I want more than that. I want to be *really* illuminated, like Angela was."

My eyes drifted over to the hammered copper urn of stones that sat on the floor next to my chair. A charcoal-gray rock lay on top. I picked it up and plunked it down next to the flickering globe on the center of the hassock between us.

"I've got a question for you, Sandy. Does this rock have any light in it?"

She looked back at me. "Well, I don't know. I wouldn't think so." She turned to point at the candle. "But for sure that's the kind of light I want."

I knew immediately where we were headed.

I began by sharing with Sandy what I learned about light from the wisdom keepers I met in my travels.

"In our culture, we're used to talking about light and dark as two separate forces. The indigenous sages I've worked with don't sort it the way we do here. They say there's no absolute darkness. Their experience is that there's only light, just greater and lesser expressions of it." I took a breath. "You've seen the yin-yang symbol of Taoism? There's a dot of light in the larger half of darkness, and a spot of darkness in the light side? Sort of like that."

Sandy looked at me intently.

"I think you're forgetting something you already know. Here's another way of putting it. When you're preparing for a romantic night with your fiancé, do you dim the lights or switch on a floodlamp?"

"Wow, I get your point," Sandy replied.

"Well, what would it be like in your next training if you carried in the idea of brighter and lesser light being equally beautiful expressions?"

The clock on the wall made a few ticks as she thought. "This is ... big," she said slowly, as the impact of the insight and question set in.

I reached over and gently pushed the gray stone closer to her. "It makes me wonder whether the bright light you attribute to your mentor has less to do with how brilliantly she shined and more to do with her ability to value the dim. Maybe so others around her could more easily come to recognize their own bright light?" I suggested softly.

A couple of lone tears slid down Sandy's grieving cheek. "You know, it's true," she said in a different kind of hush than before. "Not only did she do that in the year she coached me, but she physically dimmed as the cancer progressed and her acceptance was extraordinary. It was like watching someone slowly vanish and become nothing but graceful elegance." The tears rolled faster now.

"Sandy, we've all got to work with the light *and* the less light to fully express all of who we are. What does it matter if we're 'illuminated' if it means we need to separate ourselves from the down, dirty, and discarded to do it? Isn't 'enlightenment' the direct experience of seeing through the illusion of good, better, and best? Plus, we need density and heaviness to bring all that enlightenment down to the details and circumstances on the ground of life ... or ... well ... what would be the point?" I didn't expect an answer; I was speaking out loud for both of us, not just for Sandy. Or myself.

In that moment, time began to dissolve in the room and a quiet still space emerged between us. We sat paused, almost breathless, between silent emotions that felt like contractions marking an imminent birth.

"Sandy, what do you think stands between you remembering that you're already the world-class coach your mentor knew you to be? Is there a story you think is in the way?"

"Well, that's easy. It's scarcity," she replied. "I can still remember being thirteen or fourteen years old and sitting down with my siblings and having our parents tell us, 'We don't have enough. We're not going to be able to put you through college. If you want a car, you'll have to get a loan or figure out how to do it all on your own.' I have this feeling that there's never enough and I have no support. That's exactly what stands between me and my desire to be a world-class coach."

This was my lead-in to connect our conversation about light with her judgment about herself, her family, and the experience called scarcity, as if it were an example of a terribly unenlightened condition.

I needed to create an experience for her to step into.

I asked Sandy to look around the room, to find something that felt like it represented her story of scarcity.

She immediately focused on a bronze sculpture in the corner. The jaguar was slinking out from behind a peace lily plant and seemed to be about to take a turn in our direction. The cat was quite lifelike. It carried a fierce stalking expression as if on a hungry prowl for its next meal. Sandy shuddered. "While it's a gorgeous piece, I sure don't like the look of it," she said as I walked across the room to pick it up.

"Great," I said. "Let me bring it closer."

The jaguar's long, heavy body was taller than the hassock that held the stone and the light. I leaned it upright against the leather footstool, its front paws almost scratching at the surface of the hassock for real. Its carved eyes stared into the glass globe, seeming ready to devour the flickering light of the candle.

Just like death did with Angela.

With tears in her eyes, Sandy said, "That's it. That's the picture of scarcity right there. I hate it. It's about to extinguish the light of what I want and the support I need to get it. It puts me into a state of complete and total fear." Her voice quivered as she continued, "That fear *is* the scarcity I feel. It's definitely what's blocking me. The jaguar embodies it."

The emotional contractions in the room were coming closer together now.

"Sandy, what happens when something becomes scarce?"

Tears continued to roll down from her eyes. "It's all about survival. If I didn't have this family history behind me of there not being enough, always on the brink of survival ..." Her voice trailed off, eyes fixed on the jaguar and candle.

"Try it on this way and see if it could be a fit. When something is scarce, it becomes precious. Do you remember what you said when you first sat down on the couch? You said you were hungry to become a world-class coach, hungry to emanate the same kind of light as your mentor." I paused for a little bit to give this form of hunger game we were playing time to sink in.

"What if instead of condemning scarcity, you went after it as something precious? What if you let yourself become so hungry that you decided to feed on preciousness ... the preciousness of the dim and the bright, the preciousness of all aspects of life itself? Isn't that what Angela lived? Isn't that how she thrived, right up until her death? Isn't that what you're seeking to share in bringing your work globally?"

I motioned for Sandy to come to the other side of the hassock and place her hands on the rippled bronze form of the jaguar's body, steadying it as it honed in on its prey.

She walked around, knelt to the floor, and grabbed its torso.

"Hold onto her, Sandy. Merge with her. Tap into your own hunger, hunt the scarcity, the preciousness in every-thing, and don't let anything get in your way." I offered as I came behind her and placed my own hands on her shoulders.

In that moment, we became a three-headed predator that wouldn't stop until everything was devoured.

I once heard it said that true freedom isn't liberation *from* something else. True freedom is the recognition that everything seemingly outside of us is contained inside of us. In that moment, we were all one: the globe of light, Sandy the global coach, her mentor, the jaguar, and I.

Chapter 11
Enter the Womb

When we are truly in a spirit of adventure, we are moving just like this child. Full of trust, out of the darkness of the forest into the rainbow of light, we go step by step, drawn by our sense of wonder into the unknown.

Adventure really has nothing to do with plans and maps and programs and organization.

Osho Zen Tarot, Adventure card

used with permission

ɞ

Behind the chest-high reception desk, Katey sat on a chair in front of her computer. Her daughter Grace was balanced cross-legged on her lap, looking directly at Katey, whose face was lit with the kind of affection and joy that only a child can bring a mother. Grace's body eclipsed the view of patient data on the computer screen behind her, vying for her mom's fullest attention in great exaggeration. It was a playful moment and endearing to witness.

"I don't get these moments too often anymore," my colleague Katey joked, as if talking to me about a too-busy toddler catching a brief rest on her lap. "I've gotta enjoy them while I still can," she laughed, re-shifting her weight on her chair as she crossed her arms around her daughter's back.

Katey and I shared an office. She asked me if I'd work with her daughter Grace, who recently returned from her first year at a California college. When I walked through the office door, I found them in this sweet and unusual embrace.

While exchanging a hello and how are you, and before Grace carefully stood so neither of them would get seriously hurt, I saw it. Grace briefly disappeared. I was left looking at a strange sort of living sculpture of a Madonna and unborn child. Katey's arms no longer clasped her daughter, but hugged an imaginary pregnant belly that appeared to contain an enormous being—apparently, one who was nineteen years overdue.

This didn't register at the time with any direct understanding, nor did I assign it any particular meaning. It was simply a signpost for later attention to file in a personal storage area that acts like my very own third-eye Cloud.

As a midwife of perception, I've learned to pay attention to what arrives in the receiving blanket of what I see in the first ordinary moments, or hear in the unconscious small talk, with my clients when we meet. It's the first glimpse of a kind of premature birth, delivered in tiny ways easily overlooked and always ahead of schedule. It arrives before they've had a chance to explain what brought them to my door, as if their unconscious actions are a bundle dropped by a surreptitious stork onto my office steps.

These observations or comments scream at me like the first sounds echoing from a delivery room, giving me a chance to glimpse what has either been germinating in my clients as a condemning judgment sorely in need of air or a forgotten resource of wisdom that can't wait a moment longer in restraint, so they're supported in living a fuller and more vibrant life.

Could it be that the soul knows it's about to be heard and has to drop an early clue, while the rest of us in the room catch up to recognize the hint as it unfolds over time?

These small telltale signs have been deeply swaddled, which is why they're often so easily missed. It's as if they've been hidden from view in a game of hide and seek we all agree to play during the span of our lives, so we can discover meaning later, at the perfect time.

That is, of course, if we're watching and listening.

Back on her feet, Grace greeted me with a big hug. From there, we walked together to my office, where she plunked herself into the soft dark-purple chair to the right of mine. She sat sideways, angling herself to face me more directly. After a few minutes chatting about school and summer, I asked her why she came. Grace let out a long sigh, leaned back in her chair, tipped her head up to the ceiling, and said: "I've never felt so unsure and confused in my life."

I'm always stunned when teenagers and young adults appear to feel like life has already gone on forever, especially compared to when the elders of us feel it's so incredibly short.

"Okay, so close your eyes, Grace. Is there an image that comes along with that unsure and confused feeling?"

"Yep," she replied almost immediately, "a black void." After a short pause, she opened her eyes and made an announcement. "I'm taking a year off. I don't want to go back to school. I think I'm going back to California to live with my aunt and establish residency, so I can go to school cheaper later on. I really need to finish school, but I don't have a plan. I have no idea what I want to do. I'm *so* confused." Grace threw her arms up toward the ceiling.

She went on to tell me about her fear of getting stuck in a job and being unhappy, like one of her high-school friends who didn't go to college. She was sad that her friend had dropped her love of dancing, too tired after working all day at the physically demanding job she'd taken to support herself. Her friend felt she had no choice. She had to give up dancing and focus on what she *had* to do, rather than what she *wanted* to do.

The bane of *should* begins to chase us early in life.

"Grace, what makes your heart sing? What do you really love to do?"

She thought for a minute. "I don't know. All I really like is baking and traveling. But I have no idea how that fits into anything. I feel like I *should* have a plan. That's why I'm so confused. I have no plan. Just a black void."

"So follow that for a minute, Grace—baking and traveling. If the two went hand in hand, where would they take you?"

Grace began to tick off options, quite a number for someone so certain she was in a black void. She talked about doing transient work on organic farms out west or maybe even Hawaii, or cooking for international guests at an exotic retreat center. There seemed to be lots of possibilities alongside the *shoulds* she feared might lead the pack. But none had any real oomph behind them.

While Grace may have come looking for a particular solution to what she perceived as a problem, something else was definitely at play, an opportunity showing up in the form of this specific dilemma. The answer wasn't about leaving my office to go hunting on the Internet for jobs in destination locations. It went deeper than that.

She would surely stumble upon the same place again in her life, probably in much more challenging circumstances, if we didn't get as close as we could to the source of what was happening to discover what was there. My job was to listen far upstream.

Grace had named it pretty quickly. She called it the black void and I saw it peering out from a fold in the swaddle. She wanted to know how to bring together the elements of not knowing and not seeing, maybe never being able to see, with the desire to know.

Even at the tender age of nineteen, Grace was no different than the rest of us. Perhaps the biggest angst of the human experience is the dissonance response when we don't or can't know or see an outcome.

Grace brought to mind a client who lived in tremendous anxiety over his health. His suffering could only be quelled by a diagnosis, even when what was identified would've given someone else a far greater "cause" for worry. Not knowing was far more threatening to him than knowing. He was the opposite of those who treated denial as a friend. He lived in the epitome of "what I don't know *will* hurt me."

"Do you use a recipe when you bake, Grace? Or do you like to make it up as you go?"

"I like both."

"Perfect," I said. "That's half the battle right there."

"In what way?"

"Well, there's a time for each kind of approach. We can choose what we want to bake, follow a recipe, and get expected, tried-and-true, consistent results. It works. We can also start completely in the dark and co-create something with our ingredients that either becomes delicious or fails wildly. That's a possibility too. But that's what great chefs have to do. Are you up for something like that?"

At this point, Grace seemed intrigued, especially because I was using what she named as her passion to illustrate my point.

We began talking about planning versus stepping into the void and working in the darkness. As we talked, I reached over and picked up seven or eight tiny round pieces of raw amber that I keep beside me to the right of my own purple chair. I moved the leather hassock between us and started placing the yellow-gold nuggets on either side of the footrest's main seam, as if they were a series of footprints or stepping-stones.

Grace leaned over to look closer. "What are you doing?"

"A good friend of mine taught me something really important about what we're discussing here. I was with her when she was climbing a set of stairs. She's got a spinal condition that makes walking, particularly climbing, a real challenge. That day, she'd done a lot of walking and was really tired and in pain. She described her experience on the stairs to me like this. When she took a step, she had no real idea of how, or even if, she would land on the next one.

She experienced the process as if there were no step ahead of her. When her foot left the stair she'd been standing on, it seemed to vanish. Then the next step seemed to simply appear." As I narrated my friend's experience, Grace listened intently.

I went on to recount for her what my friend told me she discovered that day—that she felt like she was walking truly in the present, completely supported, but with no past behind and no future in front of her. The steps appeared only as she needed them to appear; they disappeared the same way.

"So, Grace, that's kinda what my little map here shows. It's very different than what we normally do when we plan and aim for a particular target. It's taking a step from the security of what's known into the void where nothing can be known. Then the next stepping-stone appears to support us. Mostly what we do, in our culture anyway, is to plan steps, to make certain we see them before we reach for them."

I could see Grace's wheels turning.

"Don't get me wrong; that's a great way to be. It's wonderful to have goals and mobilize our resources a hundred percent behind them. It's like making a tried-and-true recipe that delivers predictable, desired results. But this ... This is a different way of moving forward." I continued to place the translucent amber pebbles, one by one, on the footrest. "The cool thing is that this way is full of surprises and can bring things to you that you might never imagine possible."

I didn't mention it out loud to Grace, but as I sat there, I remembered the time ten years earlier when, shortly after completing my own training, I was asked to join my teacher at a weekend program he was delivering, so I could act as a liason to participants.

Of course I said yes, believing I was going to pass out brochures on break and get a mini-vacation from home at the same time.

So when I found myself sitting in silent terror in a circle of 75 people at 8 p.m. on a Friday night when my teacher was nowhere to be found, it was, to say the least, a surprise. The panic worsened *after* he arrived ten minutes past the start time of the program and introduced me as a member of the teaching faculty at the school. If I'd been asked directly to assist him, I would have politely refused, certain I wasn't ready. I wouldn't have been able to see it as possible. But for the next two days, he proceeded to toss me the ball in the form of demonstrating various exercises and having me lead pieces of the work for participants.

I was thrown into the ring of fire and not only didn't I see it coming, I couldn't have. *Had* I seen the next step before it appeared in this way, I never, ever, would have agreed to go.

His ability to see something in me before I could see it for myself set a new cycle in motion. I wasn't following a recipe of steps to become a teacher; it came completely out of the blue. Yet what he saw was there all along.

It occurred as magic.

In this moment, I watched Grace in front of me, her head slowly nodding in agreement as she looked down at the hassock. She showed all the same signs of discomfort as I did that weekend. But something changed while she watched me lay down the little gold-like nuggets.

"But Pat, how do I do that? It's totally scary to be in the dark about things."

No reply was my reply.

"Wow, weird. Like right after I asked you that, I had

a flash and remembered something. For a while when my brothers and I were little, we shared a room. We'd all be lying there ready to go to sleep and my mother would tell us stories in the dark. Later on, like a couple years later, I always needed a nightlight on in order to go to sleep. But before that it was great. The dark was really comforting. I could feel my mom with us."

That was when the Madonna and unborn child stored in the third-eye Cloud downloaded. Whoomp! And there it was.

I'd seen it in the waiting room soon after I walked in. Grace was inside her mother's womb in total darkness. The pure love, joy, and comfort it gave them both to remember that embrace defied time and physicality. In a silly moment behind the reception desk, they were living out a source of universal memory that persists even long after any of us still have a mom to physically hug.

But Grace, like most of us, was distant from this memory. We've collectively forgotten we can trust the darkness.

"You know, Grace, that story is exactly what you need to remember now. The darkness contains everything you need and lots more that you can't imagine. If you stay connected to your passions and focus on what you love, what you've been calling the black void will mix with them to create something amazing. Work to remember the dark as a place of comfort, like it was when you were in your room with your brothers and a little while ago, when you curled up on your mom's lap like you were inside her womb."

I pointed to the photograph hanging on the opposite wall of my office, a telescopic image of the Pleiades constellation. "Do you like sunsets, Grace?"

She nodded.

"Well, the next time it's a clear night, go out at sunset and look up. After the sun dips below the horizon and the sky goes dark, watch the stars begin to appear out of nowhere," I pointed down to the leather hassock, "just like the stepping stones that appear out of nowhere when we're willing to walk into the void and don't know where we're going. Your mom's boyfriend is a sailor, right?"

"Yes, he is."

"Ask him about how sailors navigate. They make their way in the dark using the stars. It's the planning of the adventurer. It's not better or worse than using a good recipe for something you can rely on to turn out well. There's a time for that kind of planning too." I got up to pull out my massage table, so she could stretch out on it and go on a journey. "We just want to become really comfortable with both."

On the table, I wanted to give her a silent and deeper experience of what we'd already discovered together, so she could record it in her cells using her own breath.

The whole process of the cycle of human breath is about bringing light into darkness and recycling it to come up and out once again.

Grace climbed on the massage table, looking up as if stretched out for a planetarium tour of the universe. She was ready to explore, well-prepared for the dark void to become a home for adventure, step by step, breath by breath.

Chapter 12

Eat or Be Eaten: Holy Communion

The first fish I caught was a sunfish.

They were an easy catch at the lake, flapping fast to the surface on hooks baited by my older cousin John who, unflustered and casual, placed worms onto the sharp-edged snares at the end of my lines.

He seemed impervious to the violent nature of it all, which was so starkly apparent to me as a small and curious observer. Yet the thought of being an accomplice to a potential killer didn't keep me from standing at the lake's shore in the early morning and at dusk, casting into the center of rippling targets of water that marked the place where what lives in the deep meets the surface in an instinctual drive to eat.

Or be eaten.

I imagine now that to the watchful eyes of the adults glancing through the windows that lined the back of the cottage, it must've appeared unusual to see a little girl derive such satisfaction from carrying a fishing pole, enjoying the continual play of casting out and reeling in. But even if they weren't surprised, from their perspective they might have missed the curious balance in a joining of this kind, the enchantment and revulsion that operated side by side in this sacrificial game of bait and catch.

Or perhaps they did see it. On a fundamental level, everyone plays with the swing of seeming opposites. Advancing and returning comprise an ageless dance with infinite expressions. Everything emanates out and eventually returns home again. It's the breath and essence of all life, an ever-flowing, sacred change of direction by the One.

According to my cousin John, all the fish I caught were too small to keep. So the wide-eyed, bloody, and maimed were thrown back into the water. The less fortunate that didn't survive the pole-and-line struggle were tossed into a plastic bucket in the sand beside the lake. I had no idea of their fate.

When I hooked a rare bass a couple of summers later, I was introduced to another level.

I was nearly pulled into the water by the strong tug after casting my line from a rowboat captained by John. He'd paddled us across the lake to the rocky edge of the opposing shore where a small waterfall spilled into a stream that emptied into the lake. There, with a mix of pride and nervous adventure, I finally reeled in something worthy of keeping.

After the row back to the cottage, the bass lost its blood and bones when John chopped off its head and fileted the meat with the same callous disregard he had for worms. Once again, I was at his side, mesmerized and aghast by my front-row seat where all the gore played out on the stage of an old splintered picnic table. What became unrecognizable from the original catch was stored for the night in the refrigerator.

The next morning, John's mother, my mother's cousin whom I called Aunt Honey, prepared the bass in a puddle of butter. She cooked it in a cast-iron pan over a gas flame in the cottage kitchen of the home they all referred to simply as The Lake.

It was no ordinary breakfast.

I sat alone on one of the two benches that stretched alongside the long plank table that gathered John's family—five kids, two adults—during summers away from their city home in Bayonne, New Jersey.

"When I'm out here for the summer, I miss our church and being able to walk down the street to receive communion every day," Aunt Honey's voice trailed off behind a clatter of dishes as she spoke to my mother.

I could hear their voices through the paneled wall that separated the dining area from the kitchen, while I waited to eat what I killed, but never directly touched. My hands were clean in more ways than one, since others around me did the messy bidding of death on my behalf, save the cast-and-reel participation of my push-button plastic rod.

At the time, I sensed and stored the importance of the moment, though many decades would pass before I fully understood what occurred when the plate arrived, and I finally lifted the fork into my mouth and swallowed the soul essence of *fish*. Spiced with a little salt and peppered with equal delight and horror at this culminating drama, the fish and I were together again, at home in each other.

It raised scales at the back of my neck.

Much later, after another spiritual union via prepared fish, I looked back at the great catch of the large-mouth bass and my tomboy summers at The Lake as one of the early clues that vast intelligence and enormous heart are ever-present in ordinary things, a kind of living wisdom that can take a lifetime to recognize and appreciate, if ever.

More than forty years later, this time in the high desert rather than beside a New Jersey lake, my seat was on a meditation cushion rather than a hard wooden bench. Even though I sat in perfect stillness, my mind busily scratched graffiti over every inch of white adobe wall in the Taos zendo. To the left of the kiva was a list of what I'd eaten for breakfast. On the right was what I hoped would be for dinner. There was no moment of Zen peace, no prolific narrative to follow when my eyes opened, pen poised to receive the next writing prompt. There was only an insatiable mind concerned with the memory of my most recent meal and the imagination of the next. I was defenseless against an onslaught of thought-warriors dressed as turkey sausage, warm bread, and hot coffee.

I hunted the cause, nose to the ground, sniffing for the beginning of my war against hunger.

I'm told that when I was a baby, my mother, driven by a sense of efficiency and a distaste for messiness, fed me by hovering a spoon in front of my lips, always ready to deliver the next bit of applesauce before I'd swallowed the last. There were no games of choo-choo train, no Gerber airplanes, no opportunity to wrestle tiny keepsake silverware in chubby hands or smear strained plums like finger paint. There was only my mother's persistent spoon—and my indictment of her for creating one of the things I liked least about myself: my insatiable appetite.

At least that was the way I told the story until I traveled from Connecticut to New Mexico to attend a silent Zen writing retreat with Natalie Goldberg, equipped with a notebook, fast-moving pen, and enormous expectations.

With naiveté as my carry-on, I flew nearly two thousand miles to sit cross-legged atop a cushion in a meditation hall at the base of the Sangre de Christo Mountains to follow my breath all the way in and all the way out. I thought these would be the ideal conditions to open a floodgate of words that would spill over the dam and arrange themselves in neat chapter order. Yes, I'd come to Taos to give myself over 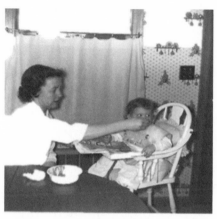 to a book that was stalking me. At the time, I had no clue what the book would be about, so I hunted the answer to that question as it haunted me, continuing to be disappointed by every word that emerged. All I could see was my mind's a la carte menu on the adobe wall in front of me. All I sensed was a continual preoccupation with being really *really* hungry.

It never occurred to me that what I sought was already in plain sight.

Three days in, after the sound of a gong marked the break for lunch, I set down my spiral-bound notebook and walked to the dining room with half-numb legs, worn, battle weary, and starving. I plopped in defeat into an old, straight-back, wooden chair that was a little too tall for the table's height. After pulling myself in close, I flashed back to the wooden high chair I sat in as a toddler, the seat where I was trapped to face my mother-blame and the perceived weapon of her hovering spoon.

I glanced around the silent table and watched fellow retreaters moving as slowly as they did in the zendo. An invisible cushion of thick air surrounded their bowed heads as they studied the laminated cards stationed near their plates. Each card sported instructions about eating with gratitude, chewing mindfully at least thirty-five times before swallowing. It was the supposed hallmark of the Zen eater, a practice that would support the Zen writer during the next twenty-minute writing prompt after lunch.

Fatigue and frustration assured I no longer cared whether I stood out from my more mindful peers. Ignoring the card, forgoing both fork and spoon, and bypassing the standard politeness to spread my linen napkin across my lap, I reached down with both hands and took a large, unZen-like, two-fisted bite of my lunch.

I was unprepared for what I discovered hidden inside a pair of innocent-looking Tex-Mex tamales. But there, buried between layers of tilapia and ancho chiles, was the overlooked gratitude for the single most precious gift a mother could give to her child: an insistence to eat everything on the plate.

It rose up in familiarity from the soul essence of fish, along with my awkward high chair in the dining room across from the zendo, and released fifty years of tears. My mother literally filled me with a key wisdom teaching, without either of us knowing it, until that moment when I realized that the quickest way to delve into the Oneness of what joins All is to eat. Eat everything. Eat every bit the Mother gives and make it a holy communion.

Suddenly, my mother-blame melted and dissolved into a lake of appreciation.

If I'd been bold enough to break the vow of silence I made when entering this five-day retreat, I would've shouted to the others that not only was I in contact with a new vision of my own mother, I could hear the voice of the Mother-Of-Us-All coming from beyond the walls of the Mabel Dodge Luhan house. It erupted out of the sands of the desert that rolled to the base of the Blood of Christ Mountains to deliver a message of urgency: Treasure your appetite and eat even what you turn away from. As long as you add love, you can eat it all. I could hear her words echo in the silence.

"What you seek is already right in front of you, no matter what you encounter. Accept it. Join what's outside with what's inside. There is both all the difference in the world and no difference at all. Reject nothing—bitter, sweet, sour, savory, or salty. Swallow it. Transform it into a digestible form. Allow it to become the fuel for living the most extraordinary life. Nothing has been offered at this worldly feast that's not Holy."

The scales that rose on the back of my neck were now the scales of balance, the measure of wholeness and Holiness in all things.

Chapter 13

Make a Difference

One morning not long ago, my eighteen-year old son Lucas plopped into a chair at the kitchen set my parents passed along from my childhood when my husband and I were first married. Though I never liked the style, it was hard to part with the stored sentiment and years of overheard conversation that lived deep in its wood.

"Take your elbows off the table. Take your feet off the rungs of the chair."

The fifty-year-old voices that never saw me in quite the right place back then still echoed off the maple finish in early mornings when our kitchen was quiet. Funny how, despite all the years of apparent mishandling, the table and chairs were never as fragile as my mother insisted.

My son looked up at me with a confident smile, his baseball cap obscuring the tops of his eyes in such a way that I wondered if he could ever really see anything directly in front of him. But this morning, he was clearly seeing something. His self-assurance, combined with folded arms and the long stretch of his crossed legs, gave it away. He cleared his throat before speaking, a little twinkle in his eye.

"You and Dad raised us without values," he stated with the certainty of a first-year college student starting to make his own way in the world.

I nearly choked on the handful of almonds I was popping into my mouth.

You've got to be kidding me, I thought. *The two of us? Gave you no values?* My mind immediately dismissed the idea, as minds tend to do, while I swallowed.

But it was a rare interchange with a young man who could go several days at a time without offering a recognizable syllable as he passed in frequent relays from the refrigerator to his second-floor cave. So I paused, pretending to have only a casual interest in what he was saying, in order not to scare him back up the stairs with too much attention.

"Really? How's that?"

"Well, maybe it's not that you gave us *no* values, but there was never anything specific. I mean, c'mon, Mom, we even went to a *Unitarian Universalist* church. Everything was always about being open and accepting." He flung his arms wide for exaggerated effect. It was hard not to laugh.

"Well, *that's* a value, isn't it?" I asked, hoping for a little something out of the categoric dismissal.

Despite the playfulness of the conversation, I wasn't fully present to what Lucas was trying to say. I was too busy constructing a number of defenses to prove that we were good value-providing parents after all. Though I was a great listener for a living, apparently I sometimes missed the mark with friends and family. It wasn't until a few months later that I could really dig into the offering in Lucas's statement that day—wisdom I totally missed at the time.

I needed to wait until my world was fragile enough to break through the wrap of perceived wrongness so I could see what was underneath all along. I had to lose the ring of the its-your-fault-because-you-did-this-to-me mentality. Letting go of my own certainty that criticism was Lucas's intent, or accepting it even if it was, allowed me to look into my own sensitivity and the spirits of critique that entwined themselves around me for too long to admit.

Long enough to still be held by the rungs of old kitchen chairs.

It was time to submit to the demons of sensitivity that chase me wherever I go, desperately begging me to stop and be with them, while I run around seeking some substitute connection instead, pretending they're not enough.

I wonder how often I've missed opportunities that were right in front of me, how often I wore a hubcap, instead of a baseball cap dipped below my own eyes, cutting off my view of unique people, places, and circumstances simply because I couldn't recognize them apart from the spinning wheel of my own personal universe.

Lucas, in the end, was right. The value of the All was the resounding message my husband and I delivered. Our extreme views and their varying derivatives drove our lives in magnificent ways, while unconsciously creating the opposite in a never-ending game of hide and seek. We were a family who spoke fluently of community and sometimes lived in secluded grottoes much like Lucas's cave on the second floor. More often than not, we were *All-consumed.*

Two months after the conversation with Lucas, on another quiet morning while showers of rain hit the sky-lights in the sitting room nearby, I was pelted by a parade of visitors hovering in the door. Though they were as real to me as Lucas was weeks before, they were the demons that took shape in the vulnerable, opportunistic moment of a rainy Thursday, insisting they would no longer be dismissed.

Next to one of the French doors was the apparition of a friend who recently retracted a commitment he'd made to one group of friends in favor of being together with feathered others from a different flock.

Next to him was the face of an old friend whose professional motto was to "make a difference" for others. While I admired my friend and the results his work produced, I often judged his approach in our relationship, personally experiencing him as more focused on encouraging me to be like him, rather than to accept me as I was. In the moment he appeared, I saw exactly why our relationship was often a struggle. It occurred to me that I might not be seeing him accurately because of my own bias.

Next came the autistic woman from the video posted in a timely way to my Timeline on Facebook earlier that same morning. She challenged those who viewed her as non-communicative to take a deeper look at the beauty of her distinction, a way most would not acknowledge as recognizable, let alone attractive.

Then there was the woman who was an early client in my practice and later turned into a texting friend; she'd been diagnosed in her youth with multiple personality disorder. While she claimed I taught her how to see the One in the Many, which might have been true, she was the one who first offered me the gift of seeing the Many in the One. At the time, I didn't have near the capacity she did in understanding the great value in this perspective.

On and on they appeared out of nowhere, until they all crowded together and assembled as a united nation of ambassadors, something out of the land of delightful and wonderful misfit toys, asking—no, begging—me to acknowledge their differences as easily as I could acknowledge what connected them.

In my vivid imaginary world, I invited them to step across the threshold into the kitchen to join me for breakfast. I asked them to sit at the now semi-antique table of my childhood. I wanted them to take their own place and be whoever they wanted to be, whoever they actually were. I allowed them to put their elbows on the table, talk with their mouths full, fold their hands and say grace, do what their mothers told them, or break all the norms with their deviance and lack of manners.

It was the same kitchen table at which Lucas invited me to sit with him, but I was too busy defending against, to ever truly join him.

So together on this rainy day, the demons and I gnawed away at the All for our breakfast, finding the values that Lucas was perhaps looking for that day weeks ago when he came to connect with me while I did dishes and popped roasted almonds in my habit of making everything mine. I secretly hoped he would pass us, demons and All, on his next trip to the refrigerator.

But it was too early in a teenager's morning and a mother's mourning over lost time.

Timing being everything, maybe it was the moment for me to break another of my hard-and-fast rules and join Lucas in his own cave, in the place I mandated eating to be taboo.

He never paid attention to any of my rules anyway, being an older teenager naturally more interested in parties and peers than conversation with parents.

Maybe I should accept his invitation to party and bridge our two worlds together, Unity and Diversity.

Perhaps somehow I could value it enough to make a difference.

"Giving a Party for the Wounded Ego," by Maryann Stow

Chapter 14

Become the Sound of Music

It was far from music to my ears when I heard the tailgate lower on the landscaper's truck outside.

We'd just stretched out our yoga mats for corpse pose when the two snarling lawn tractors bounded down an iron ramp to barrel back and forth over the chemically enhanced, jungle-green grass of the property next door. The twin engines roared through the chain-link fence and again through the tiny-checkered screens of the yoga-studio windows. The sounds swallowed every inch of calm in the room, or at least every inch in me. They licked their lips after making a meal of my equanimity, before moving on to sniff at the other corpses.

Unlike the *real* end of the line, everyone taking a yoga class looks forward to this kind of grand finale, a rare opportunity to play dead. It's a quiet reward for an hour of stretching. But the breach of peace in today's class experience was a lesson in itself, a reminder that none of us is ever free from the hot breath of unexpected predators.

Humans have played the game of hunter and hunted as far back as collective memory can go. As a result, our nervous system is coded to fire off at least two popular responses.

When a predator is at our heels, we can choose to fight. I could have risen up, leaving my students behind on their mats, marched out the studio door, and tried to catch the attention of the young men who were likely wearing noise-cancelling headphones as they rode the tiger-tractors in a bubble of oblivion. I could have tried to raise my voice louder than their growls or flail my hands at them in a desperate signal to cut the engines.

But I'm not a fan of fight. While I can wage war in a pinch if necessary, my go-to place is to flee.

My relationship with fleeing began as a very young child, with legs not yet long enough to swing over the edge of a cinema seat to touch the sticky and soda-stained concrete floor. I stared at an enormous screen in front of me, watching a woman skip and spin and twirl in the middle of mountain peaks. The scene captivated me. Later, when I was old enough to understand the movie's plot, I learned that the woman was also fond of fleeing. In fact, she and her family had to flee for their lives.

> *If you're going to flee, flee for life.*
> *If you're going to fight, make it a holy war.*
> *Be a hundred percent behind whatever's there.*
> *Stay present to what's true in each unfolding moment.*

A double bonus for the whirling woman with the short blonde hair was that the hills to which she fled were beautiful. They were also alive with the sound of music.

This was the first movie I ever saw. After eating a fifteen-cent hamburger and ten-cent French fries at McDonald's, my mother took us there in the family car, a brand new burgundy 1965 Mercury Monterey Breezeway, which had an electric rear window. It was like a living room on wheels that carted us around town and carried us every year to the family vacation spot in Stowe, Vermont. Stowe was home to the famous Trapp Family Lodge, an Austrian-style chalet built on a sprawl of land that overlooked the Green Mountains. The lodge was the home of the *real* baron and baroness from the movie. They built it after the family's escape from Nazi-occupied Salzburg in a setting that reminded them of their beloved Alps.

In an early confirmation of *nothing is as it seems to be*, long before my teacher coined and shared the phrase, I discovered that the *real* Maria looked nothing like Julie Andrews. It was a shock. My father met Maria at the village church where he attended daily Mass during our vacation. When my mother brought us there in the Mercury to pick him up, he introduced us. Less than a year after seeing the movie as a five-year-old, I was stunned as I grasped the plump hand she offered down to me, looked up into her old lined face, and returned a shy and polite hello. Then I watched as she got behind the wheel of her Volkswagen Bug and drove out of the Blessed Sacrament Church parking lot onto Mountain Road in Stowe. Her two daschunds clamored to stick their brown pointy noses through the passenger-side window as she pulled out.

The *real* Maria was the sudden gale that shattered a fragile certainty that lived in me then like a dandelion puff.

It was an early blow.

Even as a six-year-old, reality was testing me. After meeting the real Maria, there wasn't much I could rely on. What did feel dependable and unmovable were mountains. The once-a-year visit to the beauty of green Vermont opened me in ways I'm sure I couldn't describe, even if I'd been old enough to articulate anything of substance. The mountains radiated all that was certain and solid, majestic and peaceful. They also served another purpose. Like Maria, the hills beckoned me as a respite. Whenever I encountered a small insult or more egregious pain as a way-too-sensitive child, I could head for the hills like she did, if only in my mind.

Whether it was the occasional curt word or the deafening silence between my parents on vacation when the Mercury quickly transformed into a kind of trapped family lodge on wheels, I could become the hunter myself and stalk peace in a vast open sky, where clouds were in reach. I gained even more skill at fleeing the older I got. It carried a tremendous payoff. But gravity being the great spoiler, or perhaps the secret star of the show I'd overlooked all along, I encountered another fact: What goes up and away will always come down and back again.

Eventually, we return to face the sound of music we run from. Fighting and fleeing are marvelous paths if we commit our full selves to the effort, especially if we engage and enjoy the choice as a holy one, rather than use it as a means to challenge or escape from an unholy predator.

A more direct path is the holy freeze where we become as vulnerable and still as a corpse and surrender to accept our fate.

It wasn't the kind of freeze born of a fearful paralysis, or the ruse where I could feign lifelessness until the two roaring predators passed me by, falling for my pretense.

Rather, it was the kind of freeze of one willing to face the music. Its value was to stay present to what was happening as it was happening—to trust and allow the sound to chew away resistance. The noise of the tractors was simply doing what it was meant to do. In that moment, it was offering me the *real* practice, which wasn't about challenge, escape, or running toward bliss.

It was, in fact, practice for a game with much larger stakes, one where the predators called illness, disappointment, hardship, and loss were certain to arrive unannounced in unexpected ways. I'd simply let them have at me, freely offering my clinging to peace, and hope of avoidance, as appetizers for the rest of my expectations that would become the predator's dessert.

As most spiritual and transformative disciplines agree, death is the necessary requirement for new life. Holy freeze is the state where there is nowhere to be but present. It is the radical acceptance that offers a gentle form of death and more direct path to union, which is the ground for new beginnings.

After a time on that summer morning in yoga class, the unholy clamor attacking us through the windows eventually merged with the throaty and atonal sounds of bija mantras emanating from the silver CD player on the floor behind my mat. Somehow, strangely, they blended together to break my barrier of resistance against the onslaught. The tick of the battery-operated clock hanging on the wall joined in as a metronome. The room swelled and shrank in a sea of sound, a chaotic and discordant rise, an unlikely harmonious fall, and an unchanging steady rhythm. I didn't know what was happening for the students, as I'd forgotten others were in the room with me.

As the boundary of my body disappeared in an apparent death, something blared to life. My heart was singing.

I became the sound of music.

Chapter 15

Consider And as well as Or

"So I guess you know from my mom that I made the decision to go to the school I told you about in our last session," Genevieve announced. She was a beautiful girl whose hair color changed almost every time I saw her. Today, it was half pink.

"Yes, she told me," I replied. "I'm psyched for you. It sounds like a really great opportunity."

Just like the character Liesl in *The Sound of Music*, Genevieve was sixteen going on seventeen. She lived with her parents and brother at the far northern end of Manhattan before reaching the Bronx. It was the perfect place for a talented, creative, and already experienced young actress to grow up.

Genevieve got involved in community theater at a young age. It was one of the activities that prepped her to apply to an early-college program in New England geared toward bright and creative kids who were a little younger than typical post-high-school students. Genevieve planned to study acting and computer science. When she arrived in my office, a combination of excitement and nervousness was building for her departure, only a month away.

While we made small talk, I glanced at the sheet of paper I ripped from a spiral notebook after Genevieve sat down. Its hanging chads waved up as if to flag my attention. I crossed my legs and propped the pad against my knee, torn paper on top, so I could hold it and Genevieve in my gaze. I had to listen to two stories, one coming from the young girl across from me, the other from a piece of paper that was talking at the same time.

Both the animated and the inanimate have stories to tell. My attention tracks things in my environment that stand out or apart, vying for attention. This is nothing different from anyone else. It's just a matter of learning to trust what is in plain view. This is really what distinguishes my work from most of the great work other people do in this field. But unlike people who are overwhelmed with a high degree of sensitivity, I am, quite luckily, mostly undisturbed by what I experience.

As Genevieve spoke about what it would be like to leave her tight-knit family and community, the paper shared its grief. It pointed out the thin, blood-red trail that traveled alongside a margin of wounds, evidence of a violent separation from the mother-notebook.

From another view, the paper's severed edges grinned up at me as if they were dying to expose the secret: that they were confetti-in-waiting. It was the same story Genevieve told—a new beginning alongside a big loss. Seeming opposites are the odd couple that travel hand in hand.

Death is present in every birth; every birth also marks a death.

"Have you picked your classes yet?" I asked Genevieve.

"Yeah, I'll be taking French and theater, and some other core stuff my first semester."

"How are you feeling about the whole thing? It's a big deal, a major change ahead. You're not even seventeen yet, are you?"

"Nope," Genevieve responded, "next month is my birthday. I'll be turning seventeen just before I leave for school. And I'm really excited about it. You're right. It's gonna be a big change. I just hope the kids I meet aren't gonna be like some of the kids I met in high school this last year. Some of them were *so immature.*"

Genevieve emphasized those last two words as she folded her legs onto the seat of her purple chair and sat straight up, clasping her hands on her lap. She'd been home-schooled until her senior year when she opted to take her final two semesters at a New York City public high school. She was disappointed with her social life there. While she went on to share those details, the paper in front of me stared back and asked if we could play Scrabble. I started tearing it into small squares.

So that Genevieve wouldn't think I wasn't paying attention as she spoke, I interrupted her narrative to provide an explanation. "I'm just doing a little set-up to prepare for a game we're going to play in a minute. Go ahead, I'm listening," I assured her, despite the fact I had no idea what the game would be other than I needed to capture the word immature for her in a way she could literally look at. I picked up the black pen next to my chair and traced a letter in the middle of each block of torn paper.

When she took a break, I asked, "So what did immature look like with your friends?"

She recounted a couple of incidents and examples. Again, I listened as I made Scrabble tiles out of the words "immature" and "mature." It was easy to hear that her description of immature was rife with judgment. Maturity lived in her as a place of pride, not unusual for a smart, precocious, creative young woman. She finished talking just as I placed a letter in the last small square of paper. I looked over at her.

"Genevieve, I know it *seems* like this is all about meeting new friends who you feel more compatible with. But just for a moment, can we look at this story as if it's not about them, but about you?"

"Sure," she replied, with a little shrug to her shoulders.

I began to lay the individual squares torn from my paper on the hassock between us.

"Here's what I hear. You've got a little tug of war going on inside you. Do you remember the song from *The Sound of Music* that Liesl and Rolf sing to each other near the gazebo?" I asked, certain she'd be familiar with the famous movie musical. "'You Are Sixteen Going on Seventeen'? It's all about that space between immaturity and maturity.

It's like there's a little spat going on inside you between *I'm mature* and *immature*. It's just that on the outside, it looks like a story about you and your friends."

"Definitely," Genevieve responded, adding, "and I'm not up for more of it after *this* year. I want to start college off on the right foot."

"So what do you see as you look at this?" I asked, pointing to the paper letters on the hassock.

Genevieve leaned forward, studying what was in front of her. "Well, the *I'm Mature* is definitely over the *Immature*, and they're separate. That's pretty much it."

I knew how the game of this work went and, apparently, so did the paper. The little square titles looked up and reminded me that she didn't need to change anything, just rearrange what was already there to give a new perspective.

I leaned forward and *saw* the tiles shuffle. "Can I move something to show you what I'm seeing and hearing now?"

Genevieve uncrossed her legs and leaned forward on her elbows to move closer to the hassock. "Of course."

"Great, I replied, "just as long as you know that this is *your* story I'm mucking with—so I want you to remember one thing. My move is only a suggestion; you always have the final move. If how I shift it doesn't feel true for you, move it back. Okay? Here we go." I reached down and swapped a few letters around. "So if we take the apostrophe out after the I and switch the E, U, and R in the second word, here's what we get":

I M M A T U R E
I M M A T E U R

"An immature *imateur*," I read off our mock game board. I put on my best French accent, pronouncing the second

word as *amateur*. It came out naturally as an appeal to
Genevieve's love of the French language.

Then, as I looked down, the paper squares suggested I
ask her another question. "Have you ever been an understudy, Genevieve? Or tried out for a lead and gotten the
understudy instead?" I was responding to the words she
gave me about one being under the other. When something
sticks out for me as I listen, I always follow it up.

"Oh yeah," she answered, leaning back in the chair. Her
rolling eyes signaled it wasn't a pleasant topic. "The show
was called *Epic Poetry*. It was kind of based on Homer's
Odyssey. I *hated* being an understudy. I wanted the lead role
really badly, but casting picked someone else for it."

"Why do you suppose you didn't get the part?"

Genevieve thought a minute, giggling before she
replied. "Funny you should ask. I think it was because the
lead looked a lot younger than I did. But she was actually a
lot older—twenty-two."

*Ah ... Genevieve lost the lead role to her rival because she
didn't look as young as she needed to for the part. While her
talent and smarts contributed to her appearance as mature, it
also set her apart. She looked down on the role of the understudy,
often given to the less experienced, less mature actor. No wonder
there was a struggle going on inside her.*

"Wow," I said. "Can you hear the subplots in your own
story? Of how maturity and immaturity live together inside
you?" I laughed.

Genevieve nodded while she looked down at our game.

"Time to lighten this one up, don't you think?" I asked
before continuing. "One of the great things about being
your age, or holding an immature perspective at *any* age, is
you get to dream big dreams. One of my teachers used to

say that in indigenous cultures, young medicine men and women are given the most difficult tasks to confront on behalf of the tribe. Do you know why?" I asked, not waiting for her reply before going on. "Because the young medicine keepers don't yet know that the tasks they're given are barely possible, at least from the elders view. You see, honey, with more experience, sometimes people think they've seen and done it all, which pretty much cuts off the creative process. Sometimes a less mature view—an I-can-conquer-anything perspective—is what it takes to accomplish what seems impossible. But in you, immaturity is tied to a real drag of a story."

"That makes a lot of sense," Genevieve replied.

It was at about that moment that the paper letters shouted at me, pointing out I hadn't followed instructions. I was still holding the apostrophe in my hand. I heard the reminder from the tiles about what I'd discovered firsthand in my work over the years.

Healing and transformation don't happen by adding something that isn't already present or eliminating something because we think it no longer has value. It's about encountering the judgment in a particular perspective and expressing it in its most exalted form, which then brings a new experience in front of us as time rolls out.

"Okay, Genevieve, it's your turn," I said. "But I think you need to find a way to use this." I handed her the apostrophe.

She reached out her hand and took the paper square. Within a minute, this is what she laid out across the hassock:

AMATURE – IMMATURE

"Yep, that's it," she announced. "I needed to make this all on one line instead of two, to bring them together somehow. That's why I made a dash out of the contraction."

This time I was the one nodding my head.

Genevieve quickly and intuitively knew what she needed to do: to bring these opposites together in her, to elevate her relationship to immaturity and hold it in a different way. She was reworking her own version of the wounds-of-separation story that the notebook paper revealed to me only forty minutes earlier.

"That's it exactly, honey," I said, thinking again about how little time it took her to get what needed to be done. "You turned that contraction into something that joins."

During our remaining time, I guided Genevieve through an internal journey, an opportunity to seed and integrate her newfound awareness. As she stretched out on my table, I asked her to envision that she was in New York City on New Year's Eve. I suggested she imagine the newly connected feeling of Mature-Immature as a ball of light. Then I guided her to lift it from the base of her spine to the middle of her brain, as if it were the New Year's Eve ball in reverse, moving from street level to the top of the One Times Square building at midnight. Over and over she looped the ball of light into strands and filaments until she playfully created herself as a sphere of light.

When she was ready, Genevieve sat up slowly and moved to take her seat in the purple chair near mine. She closed her eyes for a few moments before opening them, ready to speak.

"So, what was that like?"

She smiled. "It was cool. Two things came to me. I thought about maturity and immaturity as the Odd Couple.

It's one of my favorite movies. Even though Oscar and Felix are opposites, they really need each other."

"Yep," I agreed. "What else did you notice?"

"It was like a dance. In fact, I saw Felix and Oscar dancing to the song 'One Day More,' from *Les Miserables*," she said softly, a song that talks about not being able to live when there's separation. It was the perfect set of lyrics for a musically talented and soon-to-be theater major to hear. I looked down at the floor to the remains of the sheet of paper I ripped into the smaller squares for our game.

Confetti edges waved back up at me in celebration of Genevieve's New Year ahead.

Chapter 16

Find the Light in the Dark

After a few minutes in quiet, Ness spoke up. "You know, I ordered sparkle paint the other day."

Vanessa is a gifted acupuncturist and practitioner of Chinese medicine working in the Taoist tradition of the dragon. Over time, I came to call her Ness. During an inward journey I took on her behalf during our very first meeting, "Ness" and I came face to face and I discovered her love of the loch.

"So, Vanessa," I opened my eyes when that journey, more than ten years ago, was complete. "I saw a black water moccasin swimming deep in a lake. It surfaced a couple of times to sun itself on a rock near the shore. But it was only there for an instant before it slithered back into the water. Does that image hold anything for you?"

Ness burst into a laugh. It was the first true smile I'd seen since she walked through the office door an hour before.

At the time of that first session, Ness was in the midst of a painful divorce. Like many couples, she and her wife found themselves divided by the very things that probably first attracted them: differences in how they approached planning, money, communication, and more.

"What made you laugh?"

"Well, let's just say I'm pretty fond of swimming."

I came to find out Ness was no casual lover of the water. She owned a shiny black wet suit and donned it every May, wearing it for a month until the temperature of the lake on which she lived warmed up, and again in mid-September so she could extend the season of her often-daily swims through October. The Vanessa sitting in front of me *was* the black water moccasin, living more in the water than out of it.

Not even the New England winter could quell her instinct to remain submerged. Ness loved the cold weather, especially the snow. When she visited her family's camp in New Hampshire for a weekend, she bundled up in ski pants and the parka version of a wetsuit, dug a reverse igloo, and ness-tled inside.

In the off-season, she often spent time in the sensory-deprivation tank owned by two friends. No light enters when closed; you literally cannot see your hands in front of your face. The boundaries of the body disappear, giving floaters the opportunity to encounter their own unconscious in the dark of two feet of highly concentrated salt water. It offers the experience of both a tomb and the womb.

So much about who Ness was and how she lived traveled in the opposite direction of the norm. As a child, she was diagnosed with dyslexia, and in American culture where left-brain dominance is esteemed and rewarded, Ness lived in the reverse and as such, was considered out of balance.

One of the greatest misconceptions humanity carries is how we define balance as only being fifty percent this and fifty percent that, as if they're two independent forces capable of only going so far. In fact, my own definition of balance had shifted as my consciousness grew and I began to understand just a tiny bit more about how singularity and duality might work together.

Now, when applying this to a couple in my practice, or an individual coming solo to work through a challenge in a relationship, I jokingly forbid the use of the phrase that leads with, "If we each do our part, then ..." I refer to this fifty-fifty division as "clipboard living," where we tend to track and calculate our partner's efforts against our own tallied contributions. It's a great distraction to being present.

Instead, I suggest another kind of balanced equation: the 100%-0%.

It has proven itself the quickest path to come into balance, whether talking about partnerships or not. It also assures that the benefit of one person's journey inward always extends to encompass the other in some way.

For Ness, back then and now, there were real-time outcomes connected to being such a fan of the dark depths. Sometimes it was a challenge, for example, for her to focus on returning business phone calls or do the accounting, hampering her from contributing more fully to the shared economy of partnership.

It was the equivalent of the water moccasin visiting the sunny spot on the rock only briefly before disappearing into the water. What would make those outcomes naturally brighter was for her to hold no judgment of who she was when she wasn't in the comfort zone beneath the surface.

Ness's whole world, personal and professional, organized through her right-brain dominance. It offered her and others an experience of swimming into water with no limits, a float tank with no bounds. This made her totally who *she* was, unique. It contributed hugely to Ness's offering as a healing practitioner. She was the gatekeeper at the edge, where people could meet the depths of themselves. There was no better escort—except if you were a partner who wanted her to remain on the surface longer or a new client hoping for a return phone call.

There was no taking the water moccasin out of Ness. She was as unlikely to be coaxed to spend half her time lazing in the golden light of the sun as she was to suddenly become a snowbird, spending her winters in Florida.

Years ago, in my first meeting with Ness, I was still working primarily in a model of cause and effect, having not yet procured the ability to see her as whole in her sleek water moccasin wet suit. At the time, I planted the seed in the form of a terrestrial serpent in her energy field, an ally that was both like her and not like her in order to support her in spending a little more time on the rocks in the sun.

Being the brother of the water moccasin, the garden snake leaned her toward the light and the land. If she accepted and engaged the image, she'd set off a chain reaction in awareness that would bring about changes incrementally. At the time, it relieved some immediate tension and made her feel a bit better. It allowed her to imagine that in time, there would be light and life again after divorce, after she found someone who could help with bookkeeping and field her new-appointment calls. It was if I lent Ness something to grasp for and hold on to, in hopes she could swim with the small details of her life with the same grandness and grace that she did in the deep. Like the lines in a coloring book, a shape was apparent, even though it wasn't alive yet with hue.

Yet at the root of it, I was still another person trying to pull Ness from the great waters of who she was. I was reinforcing the deeply buried message she carried about herself: that in order to know balance, she had to become someone she wasn't. Even she believed it, to a certain extent: Down deep, a part of her didn't *fully* value traversing the opposite path of others.

While we saw each other periodically in the time since that first meeting, the way I approached my work had changed. I was far more interested in encountering my clients as they were, so together we could discover the spark of magic that was hidden in plain sight.

When Ness appeared for this particular visit, talking about sparkle paint, she seemed much happier than she'd been when we first met. Things were going really well for her. She was long over the divorce. She'd literally moved a little closer to the lake's edge. Her business met her base needs, her work with others had deepened, and while the easily dismissed details of land life still caught her up, they were the sources of smaller grievances. Still, she came to my office this particular day incredibly fatigued, in the midst of what seemed to her to be reminiscent of a bout of spinal meningitis she had years earlier.

"Can it recur?" I asked Ness.

"Sure," she said. "It's like any kind of virus. It can go dormant and become symptomatic again under stress."

The next natural question would have been for me to ask her what kind of stress she was experiencing, then to follow the thread of what created this meningitis-like fatigue and try to link it to a cause: *something gone wrong, something out of balance.*

But since we worked last, I'd put away the playbook designed to swap bad for good, and sad for happy, even when people came looking to feel better. I knew that to go seeking light when thinking the dark wasn't a good place to be only propagated more unhappiness in the longer term.

There was only one offering to make: How could the experience called recurring spinal meningitis be seen *as the healing itself?*

"Ness," I said, remembering, "we were in touch around the time you first got sick. Wasn't it around Thanksgiving? The one you hosted at your house?"

She recounted what happened some years before. She was preparing the last touches on a harvest feast when she started to shiver with a spiking fever. She thought it was from the open window in the too-hot kitchen. As sick as she was, she worked through it. It ended up being one of the most wonderful times she remembered ever having with her extended family.

"When was the last time you felt as grateful as you did that day?"

"Well, that's easy," Ness replied. "It was this past February. I was almost in a head-on collision on my way home from my office. It was pitch black. A car was coming from the opposite direction and veered toward the yellow dividing line. It came so close it sheared off my driver's-side mirror and the back door handle. Can you imagine that? The angle of the cars was enough to take off what stuck out, but not enough for a collision or to set me into a spin. The weird thing was, I was completely calm. I just pulled over, called my sister, and told her I was enormously grateful to be alive."

Despite the fact that she was emotionally calm, her body clearly registered this as great stress, which is often the provocateur for the onset or recurrence of a dormant illness.

The body doesn't sort for whether stress or change is judged as negative or positive; all change occurs for the physical body as an adjustment either way. Stress is just the point where two or more powerful forces meet. I've often thought it's why the first year of being married ranks so high on the stressor scale.

Ness's narrative was a pay-attention place for the possibility of something larger than a story of a recurring virus. Another kind of spinal engagement is referred to as a "kundalini" experience, an awakening of the spine with light.

Ness continued. "You know, it's funny. Ever since I was a really small child, I've had nightmares about what eventually happened to me that night on the road. In the dreams, I'm always driving with my family in the car, completely in the dark, and all I see are bright lights coming straight for us out of the pitch black. There's never a crash. I always just wake up and am glad to be alive, totally relieved it was a dream."

As I listened, again I remembered our first meeting: the water moccasin, the sunlight and the meeting place at the rock, the dividing line between shore and lake.

"So, if the close encounter on the road was the last time you remember feeling that familiar gratitude, when did the symptoms of the meningitis recur?"

"Uh," she began with a pause, "only a few days later. Wow, the initial illness and the recurrence both occurred around big moments of gratitude. I would never have put those two together."

The illness brought Ness, great lover of the loch, to the surface to encounter the light again. This time it wasn't from a land serpent on a sunny rock *outside of her* that she either chased or chased her as she battled resistance along the way;

it was a meeting of the light that was *in* the darkness, in a place she knew well and instinctively always dove for.

The recurring fatigue and dream were offerings to wake up to the full acceptance of who she was *as she was*—unique, and fully balanced in the 100%-0% sense. She wouldn't need opportunity disguised as divorce, spinal meningitis, or a near head-on collision to propel her into the deep to find the light that had always been in her, rather than outside of her.

The Taoist yin-yang symbol flashed in front of me. I led her over to my massage table where she could dive down into the dark and find the light that would curl up the spine to the middle of her brain, the dividing line between her hemispheres.

When she came back to the chair after the table, we sat for a bit in the gap of the dark. She was glowing.

After a few minutes, she spoke up. "I've had this crazy urge to start filling the gaps in the wide plank floorboards in my office with gold sparkles."

"Yep," I said. "Cracks of lightning. What better way to wake up and bring together what's above and below."

Chapter 17

Watch What Unfolds
Out of the Blue

Elation was in the air. Our adventure was over. We were ready to return home.

It was the eleventh and last day of our pilgrimage to the peak of Peru's holy Mount Ausangate. We were camped on the land of a local alpaca farmer who lived near the trailhead where we'd started our trek; the mountain had delivered far more than any in our small international group could have imagined. For me, the essence of the epic journey was captured best by a dream I had the last night at base camp when a small earthquake shook the ground while I peacefully slept.

In the dream, four old "paqos," ancient wisdom keepers who journeyed the same terrain centuries before, levitated in a vertical mid-air stack alongside the mountain peak. As they hovered, each held the back of a metal folding chair, the kind you might pull out at a family reunion when more than the expected number of kin show up and all the comfortable seats are taken. The image gave the term "high chair" an entirely new meaning. Without words, I was told that I could come and sit at any of the four levels I wanted.

Today, we were in the foothills for a final goodbye, building small towers of stones to mark the end of our expedition, with the intention of linking these cairns through prayer to the faraway lands we each called home. After finishing my stack of stones, I was sitting tall and cross-legged. That was when I became aware of the voice.

Keep watching the peak. A message is coming.

I sat, waited, and watched as the top of the mountain appeared and disappeared under changing cloud cover. In the high Andes, one minute the sky can be a clear azure blue. In a mere blink, billowing white clouds can bring heaven down to eye level. Or as they did a few days earlier when we brought offerings to the fire the paqos lit for us in sacred ceremony next to a glacial lagoon at 15,000 feet, charcoal clouds might swallow the landscape just as fast. On that day, wind and lightning were a humbling reminder of how the larger, powerful forces of nature are always in charge.

Now, I kept watching as puffy clouds quickly exchanged shape in a forward reel. When it finally appeared, it took me by complete surprise. Wisps of white arranged in wide stripes over a swatch of bright sky and for the second time in a year, I found myself staring at a little blue house. The sky was the canvas. The clouds were the paint.

It was a nearly exact replica of a simple piece of artwork given to me by a student six months before: a square box house with a triangle roof filled in with wide, blue, oil brushstrokes. It was a gift to commemorate teaching my teacher's program out of my own home, after many years of traveling to other venues to deliver it.

The blue-and-white cloud rendering lasted about ten seconds before dissolving into new shapes.

After returning home from that life-changing expedition, reality reassembled in unexpected ways. In one of them, less than three months later, the image of the house made a third appearance. It was at the dinner table on Christmas night.

Our family was gathered at my sister's for the holiday. It was the last time we would celebrate in her house, which she was selling. The eight of us gathered around the table that night began our dinner with a tradition we'd followed for years. After a blessing, we opened a bottle of wine and the party favors my sister always bought to place on our plates. I was expecting to find silly tissue-paper crowns or the usual variety of surprise charms like the ones I found at the bottom of Cracker Jack boxes as a kid.

After a sip of strong wine, I pulled apart the shiny foil ends of my own favor. Onto the holly-adorned Spode-china dinner plate dropped a small, square, blue-and-white-plastic house with a triangular roof—the same house in the painting my student gave me and that had stunned me to tears that final morning on Mt. Ausangate.

This can't be happening.

Time suspended. The sound of laughter at the table dimmed. As I looked around the table, the same plastic house dropped on every plate, though in a different color, none blue like mine.

These party favors are never the same. Each year, they've always been different. Did the assembly line worker at the manufacturing plant where they were packaged forget to mix the favors? What's going on? How is this possible?

My mind was bending. As I looked around the table, I knew that the following Christmas, not a single person would be living in the same house they were living in then. Time proved it true.

That night I had another dream.

I found myself standing in front of our first home, a small ranch we'd left seventeen years earlier after our third child was born. As I stared at tall sunflowers growing out of the stone flowerbed that lined the front, I heard a voice.

Put your house on the market. You need to move.

When I woke up the next morning, I shared the dream with my husband, starting with the party favors the night before. Then I recounted the backstory of the blue house that appeared on Ausangate in Peru and the small painting I received last spring.

"Honey, I think we need to move," I said, looking up at the ceiling in my sister's guest room. It was delivered more as a statement than a posed question. "I mean, I *really* think we need to put the house on the market." I rolled over to my left to look at him directly, wondering how he'd react to something so unconsidered.

While we'd occasionally talked about downsizing, neither of us planned for it any time soon.

"Well, it's pretty hard to refute all that," he said, being the good-natured sport he was. "It probably makes sense for lots of other reasons, too."

"There's just one thing I don't get. I can't figure out why the voice I heard in the dream said *sell your house*, because it wasn't a picture of our house now. That part makes absolutely no sense."

On the following spring equinox, we listed our house and set out to look for a new one. Like most real-estate deals, the ordeal was months long and appeared to reach a finale when we put down a deposit on a place we liked, but didn't love. We felt pressured by the buyer for our house and a contracted move-out date. So we settled for, rather than celebrated, our choice—until the home inspection revealed a deal breaker.

Minutes after the conversation with our realtor where we pulled the plug on the purchase and despite having seen every home for sale in our town in our price range in the last six months, I felt an eerie confidence about returning to the computer to start over. There wasn't a hint of regret over what happened to halt the deal. On cue and like magic, as soon as I typed in the parameters, a house appeared in the search engine that I'd never seen before. The listing was a few months old, but the price had recently been reduced, so it now fit in our search range. When my husband returned from work, I insisted we drive by it immediately.

We didn't recognize the street name, so we plugged it into the GPS. On the way there, we realized we were retracing the steps to our starter home, the one from the dream on Christmas night. As we approached the quiet street whose name we didn't recall, we found a forgotten road a two-minute walk from our first house.

Hanging from the cedar shingles next to the front door was a welcome sign with sunflowers. On the ground under the two dogwood trees in the front was a beautifully landscaped stone compass with eight cardinal and ordinal points stretching out from a sculpted, grinning sun in the center.

We didn't need to see the inside. There was no failing to recognize it. We had returned home.

Part 3

Complicated and Difficult Magic

Chapter 18

Accept the Oscar

I shot an arrow into the air,
It fell to earth, I knew not where;
For, so swiftly it flew, the sight
Could not follow it in its flight.
I breathed a song into the air,
It fell to earth, I knew not where;
For who has sight so keen and strong,
That it can follow the flight of song?
Long, long afterward, in an oak
I found the arrow, still unbroke;
And the song, from beginning to end,
I found again in the heart of a friend.

Henry Wadsworth Longfellow, "The Arrow and the Song"

❦

"How is Susan doing?" I asked Matthew as we began our phone session. I'd worked with his wife the week before, shortly after her brother died of a heroin overdose. Matthew and Susan had made many attempts to support Jeremy's recovery, which never endured between long bouts of addiction. His death was a painful loss for the entire family.

"She's doing great," he replied. "The work you two did made an enormous difference. For sure it's my turn today. The whole thing with Jeremy's overdose has affected me so much. But something popped forward I wasn't expecting in the process."

Matthew, who sought support as he made his way in the world of international sacred-music recording, had been working with me since someone suggested he enroll in a program I was offering. He was a man of enormous presence with a baritone voice and a big heart. He was a gifted singer, chanter, and drummer.

"You know, Pat, since Jeremy's death, I've been absolutely furious with my own brother, Oscar. I think I might have mentioned to you in our last session that Oscar and I haven't spoken in over two years. In fact, he hasn't come over to meet our son since he was born, which really, really hurts." His voice began to lose its bristle as he quietly added, "He used to be my best friend."

There was no doubt that his wife's loss of her only brother triggered some deep feelings in him. I let Matthew talk for a while, listening intently for his "map" to reveal itself. The human narrative, etched by the soul, never fails to tip its hand by exposing a kind of treasure map, a place where an "X" marks the spot where something of value is buried. It isn't the kind of map used to plot a path from one place to another. It's more the type found behind smooth glass in kiosks stationed at suburban mall entrances where the "X" has an accompanying message: *You Are Here.*

The words Matthew chose, the phrases he used, without his conscious mind realizing it would indicate where the treasure was concealed.

As I listened, I drew the outer circle of a bulls-eye target on a piece of blank paper in front of me. The wood of the desk was hard, so I slid a magazine from an arm's length away under the sheet to soften the impact of pen on paper. I half-noticed the portrait of an alien face peek out at me from behind the circle.

As most of us do when we're captivated by a story of a brotherly, sisterly, or spousal challenge, Matthew was busy painting a dark picture of his estranged loved one. He was reciting a list of grievances that substantiated the separation from his brother, though I asked nothing to prompt him to defend his position. As Matthew recounted their on-again off-again sibling struggle, my pen etched the names of Cain and Abel, sons of Adam and Eve, to the side of my circular target. I was thinking how timeless the stories of love, obligation, jealousy, hurt, anger, and rage were. And how they so often ended in some form of separation or death.

Matthew was scripting the account of his life with his brother as if he were Oscar's burdened parent. He spoke about always being the one to "fix" the breeches in their relationship when they occurred, to apologize, to set things right—until the cycle inevitably repeated itself.

"Matthew, what is it about Oscar that upsets you the most?" I asked the question I knew would be easiest for him to answer.

"It's his anger," he replied without effort. "I know we all get angry. I get angry too, but *his* is an unproductive anger.

He lashes out. It's not just me. He does it with others, too. He dumps on them, time after time. I can't take it anymore." Sparks of aggravation were turning to fire in his voice.

"What keeps you from accepting your brother as he is and mending the fence one more time?" I wasn't seeking a particular response. I was poking around to get him to talk more, so I could more accurately pinpoint his "location." Stories for me are like living GPS coordinates.

The tone and volume in Matthew' voice rose. "*No*," he said emphatically. "I'm *not* going to do it again. It's always up to me. I'm tired of being the one to do it. I'm sooo angry with him, Pat. It's probably best I'm not around him right now. I don't know what I would do if I was in his company. Honestly, I feel like I could kill him."

Bull's-eye. His words hit the center of my doodled target.

Besides showing me where the arrow needed to land, Matthew told me, albeit indirectly, many other things. The first was that under stress, he felt he had only two options. Neither was desirable. He could either be miserable *without* his brother or *with* his brother when, if he reached out one more time, history was likely to repeat.

By projecting it onto Oscar, Matthew also revealed the way he sorted his anger in two, the productive and unproductive, and what he thought would be his most extreme expression of unproductive anger: murder. Sensing steam rising from the well of passion that produced his anger, I followed his lead into the mist.

Or maybe, what he had missed all along.

"So, Matthew, we can go two ways from here. We can try to get you over your rage and resentment. But it seems like you've tried that approach before and it only worked for a short while. Or we can accept exactly where you are right

now and let it lead us to where things need to go. I don't
know where we'll end up, but I think we've gotta start with
where you are." After a pause I added, "One thing I *do* know,
and I think you do too. Time is short. None of us knows
how long we have. You and Susan both know what it's like
to sustain the loss of a brother. Jeremy has shown you that."

Quietly, from the other end of the phone, Matthew
added. "Yup. And *he* used to piss me off too. *Really* piss
me off." It was becoming clearer what his relationship with
Oscar manifested in Matthew.

Using the clues he unconsciously revealed to me in the
story he told, I had Matthew stretch out where he was and
prepared him to take a journey into what ancient cultures
call the underworld, or the subconscious. I instructed him
to metaphorically buckle up and follow my voice. I also told
him that if at any point he wanted to depart from where we
were going, he should let the sound of my voice fade and
trust his instincts to follow what images, sounds, and even
tastes occurred through his own senses. I reassured him I'd
be at his side, whether he stayed with me step by step or not.
We would create the journey together.

After we synched our breath, using a soft voice, I
guided Matthew to drop from where he was lying in his
house down into an imaginary cave. After a time stretched
out on the cold stone floor, I asked him to sit up and, in
the dim environment, feel around for a bow and a leather
pouch of arrows that he'd find to his left. I suggested he pick
them up, stand, and walk toward a soft glow in the distance
where light streamed in through the mouth of the cave.
I wasn't following a script; I was linked with him in the
realm of imagination and describing what I saw.

When we reached the entrance, I had him step out and
scan the desert vista in front of him. I connected him again

to feeling the bow in his hand and the arrows that sat in the leather pouch, propped against his shoulder.

"Matthew, in the distance you're going to see a form begin to take shape. I don't know what it will be. At first, it may be hazy. But over time, it will resolve into an image that embodies suffering and separation. But at its center, it'll carry a tiny spark of heart, as all forms everywhere carry the same essence even when they're wrapped in pain and separation.

"Maybe the form will be familiar; it might be foreign or alien. But as it begins to get clear in your focus, I want you track that spark in its center and quietly reach for one of the arrows. Position your bow. Place the arrow on the string of the bow. Connect into your own heart and the well of passion that's there. Two aspects flow from that well: anger and love. Harness the passion and power in the anger you've been feeling and join with it in the name of love. Become a killer. Merge with the impulse you've had to kill off the separation with your brother. Have no fear. No blood will spill. No one will be harmed.

"Your target is the heart of the form. Aim there and slowly draw your bow back. When you're ready, let the arrow fly. If you hit your target, watch as the form depicting separation dissolves to expose the spark of light hidden beneath the surface."

My voice trailed into silence as I created a space for Matthew to experience what occurred as he followed the instructions embedded in the language of the story he told me. When I imagined he was ready, I spoke again. "Did you hit your mark?"

After a short pause, he said, "Yes," in his mellow baritone.

"Now I'd like you to walk toward where the form was. Kneel and begin to search the sand for the spark that has fallen to the ground. When you find it, I'd like you to feed it with your breath. Blow on it three times. Fuel the fire, so the spark bursts into flame."

Before long, I heard Matthew's breaths. I knew then that I wanted to lead him through a process we had shared before in a group setting, a fire ceremony.

"Reach your hands toward the flame and bring the light of love to your belly, your action center. This, too, has two aspects to its nature, doing and non-doing. Draw love to them both." I paused as he did so. "Now reach forward again and take the light of love into your own heart, bringing it to your feeling nature, where you give and receive love." I paused again. "When you're ready, draw the light from the fire in front of you to your forehead, the place of mind and thinking. Bring the light of love to all the polarities: knowing and not-knowing, the certainty of the master and the uncertainty and openness of beginner's mind."

In the silence that followed, I felt Matthew completely with me, and waited.

After a time, we retraced his footsteps. I took him back to where he lay across the cave floor, guided his consciousness back to join his body and mind in this time and place, and finally clapped him "awake."

While he returned fully to the present on the other end of the phone, I started doodling again, reshaping the edges of the dark bulls-eye in the center of my paper and turning it into a heart. Behind it, the alien face stared through the paper. After a time, I spoke up. "So what's happening, Matthew? Were you able to stay with me or did you go off on your own?"

His reply was equally soft. "No, I followed you all right, but we weren't alone. We had company." His voice began to crack. "Jeremy appeared in the cave and joined us."

Now I could hear him crying on the other end of the phone.

"But that's not all. Pat, about a month before he died, Jeremy gave me a gift. It was the only gift he ever gave me in the whole time I knew him."

"What was it?" I asked.

"It was a book," he said, sobbing. "*The Zen of Archery*. He knew I was thinking about setting up a target on our land at the new house." The synchronicity among Matthew and Jeremy and me in the underworld was a connection in deep evidence. It was breaking his heart open.

At this point, Matthew was overcome with emotion. But I had to ask one more question. "Did you hit your target? Did you take out the pain and suffering?"

"Oh yeah."

"I'm going to let you go now, so you can be present to what needs to be. I want you to stay with all that's coming up. If Susan is home, maybe you can go be with her right now. Jeremy gave her gifts too, before he left."

I paused before adding, "And Matthew? Neither of us knows what will happen with your brother. Trust your instinct not to initiate something, at least for a bit. Let it unfold. Let things reshape themselves and reorganize based on what you killed off, the suffering of separation, and the flames of love that you fanned with your breath. Let whatever arises come to you. See what happens. We'll talk in a couple of days."

I hit the call-end button on my headset and removed it from around my neck. I was misty eyed myself. The power of the unified field of experience we share—not just Matthew and I in that moment, but all of us—was strong.

It didn't really matter whether he actually re-united with his brother. He might or he might not. But whatever happened next was certain to be informed by the roll out of this experience of love. As a Zen archer, Matthew would take on the gift his brother-in-law left him, claim his mastery, and continue to aim for the heart of love. It would travel to his brother Oscar whether they mended the fence or remained distant. But the condemnation was gone.

The love would change everything. But Matthew would need to practice to perfect his aim.

I swiveled my chair and lifted my legs to rest on the desk, crossing my ankles. I looked over at the paper with my bulls-eye heart doodle and without thinking lifted the page. Underneath was the previous week's issue of the *New Yorker* magazine, which had been sitting on top of a pile of unsorted mail before I pulled it over to slip it under my paper. I looked at the strange, ET-like, golden portrait and wondered what kind of cover art the face represented. Had I missed some UFO incident in the news?

I turned to the article listings on the second page and scanned down to the illustrator's name and the title listed under "Cover." It read #OscarsNotSoWhite.

The face behind the target I drew was the golden statue, Oscar.

We couldn't make this stuff up if we tried, I thought.

But I guess if we did, it would be a production worthy of receiving an Academy Award.

Chapter 19

Enter the Fire

Fire has one hell of a reputation.

From rubbing two sticks together to spark the flame that gathers a tribe in a circle to being the main weapon in powerful warfare between warring tribes, from the flash that ignites "Creation" between the finger of God and the finger of Adam on the Sistine Chapel ceiling to the torch beneath the funeral pyre that will consume and return the dead to ash, fire has always been central to the human story. Without the fire of our sun in the sky, the warmth of the hearth, or the passion of the heart, we could not thrive. Fire can be as gentle and nurturing as a twin flame, or as fierce and ruthless as a nuclear blast.

Maybe this is why most people prefer the face of a kind and compassionate God over the fire-and-brimstone face of God.

My good friend used to wince when I made offhand remarks that encouraged the All-That-Is to bring it on. His playful plea, "Please don't say that out loud," was often a source of laughter between us, but also occurred as a nervous truth that we both knew the consequence—such as trial by fire—of invoking.

Unlike earth and air elements, which take a long time to decompose matter, or water element that transforms the material a little more quickly, fire element is an accelerant that can change things from one state to another with near immediacy. Playing with fire appeals to a rare few, those open to exploring the counter-intuitive, like the moth to a proverbial flame. Having developed a curiosity about running toward what most people flee from, I immediately connected with Peter when he first visited my office, after Laura, my client and Peter's partner, gave him a package of my sessions as his gift one Christmas.

Peter is a soft-spoken, retired, fire-protection engineer and former firefighter with a fondness for sailing and baseball. He often wears a ball cap and is in no hurry when he walks. Peter is also content where he stands. He exudes calmness and carries a wisdom that peeks through his always-thoughtful remarks.

Peter has relapsing polychondritis, an autoimmune disorder that results in a debilitating and progressive inflammatory condition. It's found in only one in three million people, so little is known about the disease. In Peter, it affects his hearing and sight and causes tremendous joint pain. Laura was concerned about Peter's physical and emotional health. When she gifted him the work, he was in the midst of a troubling flare-up.

Understanding and appreciating the body-mind-spirit connection in health, Laura was concerned Peter's illness was an internalization of trauma he carried from experiences as a first responder. No doubt there was some kind of link. This was corroborated when Peter sat down in my office for the first of three appointments: Sirens, as if on cue, were echoing in the distance.

"I'm a very lucky man," Peter began, as the wails continued softly in the background. "In some ways, I don't understand why Laura thinks I need to be here. Many times during my life, I've been accused of being rare *or* incurable," he chuckled, "and now I have a diagnosis that's both rare *and* incurable." He paused for a moment before continuing.

"I know and appreciate that Laura thinks something needs to be done about this. Frankly, it's a point of difference between us. She doesn't understand—most people don't—about what it really means to have a condition that's considered unable to be cured."

After a moment or two of reflection, Peter added, "It's another opportunity for enlightenment, I guess."

Enter fire-and-brimstone God, I thought.

While he didn't choose his medical condition consciously, it was clearly his path to awakening. Peter didn't simply contain the fire of an inflammatory condition; he'd already merged with the burning building.

I knew from speaking with Laura that her view *was* different. She linked her partner's rare inflammatory condition directly with his history and wanted to put out the fire in the man before it burned him down. It was a reasonable consideration: Laura wanted the fire*fighter* to prevail and feared he'd given up. In a certain way, I soon learned, he had.

On the heels of my thoughts, Peter continued.

"You know, Pat, there's a real difference between acceptance and resignation. I'm compelled to work with acceptance. I'm open to surprises and turns of fate, but I've already confronted the demon of my own arrogance that says I can beat anything. I've been through all of Kübler

Ross's phases of dying. I don't have past generations haunting me. I don't have spiritual baggage that's the result of what a lack of fullness breeds. Lifestyle issues certainly haven't led to this illness. The causes are multi-systemic."

I was riveted. It was rare that people came to me already accepting their circumstance. Mostly, they came in order to soften the judgments that *prevented* them from accepting what was happening. After they did, they found that acceptance naturally transports them to another place—as quickly, in fact, as fire transforms. Often, they mistakenly credited me fully for making it happen, when they were the ones who carried the spark of magic all along.

Obviously, Peter wasn't my usual client.

"In the beginning, I tried to find out everything I could. We can sit in this modern age in a library, or at a computer, and research so much. You know what I really found out from all that?"

I happened to glance over at the digital clock to my left at the exact moment Peter answered his own question.

It read 9:11.

"Nobody really knows anything," he said, with an ironically punctuated sense of certainty.

The simultaneous occurrence of his statement with the clock landed for me as an emergency message delivery.

Nobody really knows anything.

Peter was simply practicing internally what came to him naturally all of his life. He'd surrendered to his true calling.

His words were similar to the ones shared with me by a friend who was a war veteran. He'd recently been in a nursing home at the bedside of a fellow warrior as his dear friend lay dying.

"This sucks," said his foxhole buddy.

"Dying? Yeah, it totally sucks," my friend replied.

"No, not death. I'd rather be bleeding on the battlefield than bedridden in *this* place."

Like many first responders, Peter was the courageous warrior who plunged headlong into a blaze, like his brothers did on the other kind of 9/11. There was no time for hemming or hawing in an emergency, no pause to ponder choice in the usual way. He moved in the opposite direction from the survival instinct. Peter lived in a way that perfectly suited him. While it was hard for everyone else to understand, he was using it to squeeze every bit of enlightenment he could into his life, rather than being resigned to losing it.

I didn't hear the resignation Laura did. Instead, I heard acceptance.

Though listening carefully, I didn't hear any place of rejection or striving where I might echo something back to Peter to try on in a different way—until he told me a story about a tragic bus accident. Alone as the first responder on this scene, he was faced with several people who needed his help, but could only attend to one. He knew he had to choose; in doing so, others would perish. "I often see their faces in my dreams."

I *felt* his suffering and regret. Despite the fact that the fire-protection engineer in him had spent much of the prior half-hour telling me about the necessity of partnership in fire fighting, I sensed he hadn't recognized the partner that *was* with him on the job that day, even as he was alone. I guessed I might offer some wisdom for his consideration.

"Peter, I don't think you were alone that day. You *were* operating as a team … only you didn't have a partner in the usual sense. Death was a member of your squad, working side by side with you. You were simply rescuing the ones who had more time on Earth. Death was rescuing the others to bring them home." I offered it humbly, hoping this small contribution might quell any guilt that lived in him and rose during dreamtime.

"When you first sat down, you talked about the multi-systemic, how we really don't know much of anything. Maybe working consciously with death as a part of your squad might help you live an even fuller life. Maybe it can take the burden of what felt like an unfair choice out of your hands." I let him sit with this as a possibility to consider.

When Peter left my office that day, I felt a great gratitude wash over me for the Christmas gift *he'd* given *me* in our conversation. It was a corroboration of a similar message I'd received in a dream three or four years earlier, when I was called to shift the focus of my work. Like Peter, I was summoned to be a kind of first responder to the counter-intuitive at a time when our planet was in rapid transition and tottered on the brink of emergency. I was asked by the images in the dream to find deeper value in running toward what was present in circumstances when the first impulse was to run away. Its central theme was not about fire, but another vital element.

I wrote the dream down to preserve its message:

The curled wooden tip of the canoe pointed back to the center of my gaze. Spraying rapids pulled the sky and water together to meet in hasty introduction. Ahead, the powerful current disappeared past a ledge of smooth stone and dropped into a great abyss.

Even if there was time here—and there wasn't—I had no interest in shifting the course of the river. Instead, I placed my paddle in the water and sculled with one-pointed focus, adding deliberate effort to the gravitational pull of the inevitable.

Nearing the great fall, the river and I joined forces and gained unimaginable speed. I sliced across the horizon line and lifted airborne. My vessel unfurled wings.

Whether a threat appears as garden variety or epic, Peter and I answered the call in similar ways. We were first responders, and we surely wouldn't be the last.

Perhaps the count of one in three million was destined to grow, until we could all embrace the radical acceptance necessary to live fully and brightly with the passion and magnificence of the present.

Chapter 20

Shatter with Love

I tiptoe to your door
carrying a harvest basket
of soft, ripe words
meticulously picked from prickly branches
like the ones on the raspberry bush in the yard.
When you answer
I'll hide the tiny scratches I willingly endured
when I reached to grab as many as I could for you
so we could exchange them
and honor our secret agreement
to avoid remembering
that shattering your world
and our fragile view of it
is what is required for both of us to be free.

Pat Heavren, "The Eggshells We Walk On"

☙

Chris rolled his wool-socked foot in a circle over the top of the clear glass sphere. The oversized decorative bubble I instinctively packed in my belongings to bring to class raised his foot off the ground by six or seven inches. It was sitting off to his side before he reached his leg out across the carpet in a soccer-like stretch and rolled it in front of him. Inside the glass ball, two peacock feathers tumbled, the midnight-blue eye of each crisscrossing back and forth as if the pair couldn't decide on where to fix their gaze.

"It feels like the whole world is burning," he sullenly offered the group, looking down and shaking his head in a slow "no." His tone seemed to indicate there was no point in even trying to extinguish such a large fire.

It was a little more than a week after the 2016 presidential election. An air of heaviness and struggle permeated the room. From where I sat, it was hard to tell whether the upheaval was in response to the divisiveness and turbulence in the U.S. collective or parallel personal events churning internally for the program participants. Or both.

I knew Chris, for one, was having trouble finding full-time work after completing his bachelor's degree as a slightly older-than-average college student. I also knew he'd fallen for the young woman he sat next to in the first segment of our class, in September. Sara was in the process of separating from her partner when the two met. From the looks of it, things appeared to be moving quickly between them. Which likely meant swift endings paired with coincident beginnings. Without knowing any details, I imagined this was a fiery transition for both Chris and Sara.

No one in the room was spared.

Even as the leader of the program, I was processing my own inner turmoil. Rapid change rarely follows a neat agenda. As I watched the sphere and the tumbling eyes of the peacock feathers, I realized I was trying to fix my own gaze while boiling over with emotion.

As a living barometer of what stirs around me, it comes with the territory.

Hours earlier, I sat at my kitchen table in a terrible and unusual funk of resistance. I didn't want to go to the program. What I loved to do most of all in the world, teach, felt in that moment overwhelming and onerous, large and burning like the fire Chris later named. The feeling had grown out of a spark that ignited over Halloween weekend and flamed to a crescendo the night of the election.

It was after the lunch break of the October class that the first ember caught. One of the program participants sat across from me, her knees curled up into her chest in a seated fetal position.

"Julia … are you ready to share your story?" I asked, prompting her to bring her story alive in the room to explore it in a new way.

"My stomach is acting up; I *really* don't want to do this," she replied, raising her bowed forehead off folded arms.

"I get it," I responded with the kind of certainty that typically emerges when I teach. "It's because you've got a gas chamber in your belly." Even I was a little taken aback with what emerged hastily out of my mouth. It came from a place deep below the surface of my usual thinking mind.

At the time, I didn't know Julia was Jewish. Nor did I know that her grandfather was a medical doctor who attended to the physical needs of Buchenwald camp survivors in Germany at the end of World War II. I'd find out that part of the tale some months later. All I knew then was the story she told us when she rose from her seat that afternoon.

Julia was a midwife and a single mom who shared custody of her son with his father. From birth, the boy, now a teenager, grew up alternating between their two homes, which was difficult for Julia. In her heart, she sensed it was now time for him to live in one place. It was a change that would allow them both to grow.

After she finished telling us her story, I asked her to sculpt the feeling present in her body using other people in the room as props. Julia stretched her arms wide. She motioned for one member to pull her left arm and another to pull the right. It was a feeling all of us understood, being tugged in two directions. At one time or another, we'd all faced a difficult, if not impossible, life choice.

As I watched Julia in the center of the room, I saw a caricature of Meryl Streep drop in around her. It was from the scene in the movie *Sophie's Choice*, when Streep's character Sophie is ordered by a Gestapo officer to choose one child over the other to go to the gas chamber. It's one of the most horrific dramatizations of consequential choice captured in all of modern film and, perhaps, contemporary fiction, since the movie was based on the novel by William Styron. While these circumstances were certainly different than Julia's situation, it pointed to the universal struggle we all encounter when facing a difficult decision.

What we discovered that weekend was simple, yet hard to remember in the face of pain. When the pull of two directions is as strong as the simultaneous strain Julia felt on both of her arms in that human sculpture, she wasn't really in danger of splitting in two, though it felt like she might.

At the same time, the strength of the tug of war popped her heart center right out front. That was the wisdom of the body emerging, the awareness that struggle and stretch are often requirements to open the heart.

I left that weekend sparked by the power of Julia's work. It wouldn't be long, as early as the following week, before my own ability to follow the heart was tested when my own impossible choice fanned from spark into flame.

On the day of the election, I drove to my local elementary school, uncertain of how I would cast my vote. I had a preferred candidate of the two, but I also had a pact with myself that I'd only make a choice I could stand behind one hundred percent. I believed everyone else would do the same, so I could accept the outcome in trust of humanity.

For me, it wasn't only a matter of an election between two candidates. It was a choice between what they represented on a much broader scale: the familiarity of the status quo and the unexpected face of unbridled change. But it felt like an impossible choice, intensified by a growing feeling of perilous consequence. On the other hand, I also knew that what I was holding as perilous came from the bias of my own turmoil.

As I pulled up to park against the curb of the paved circle that rounded like a torus in front of the school, I looked at the American flag rising from a long pole planted in the center of a smaller, circular grass island in the middle. A swell of people stretched outside the school doors in a long line.

I sat numb for ten minutes.

When I finally stepped out of the car and approached the end of the line where giggling girls and a battalion of brownies on paper plates marked the sixth-grade bake sale in full swing, the feelings began to move in my belly. Then the polling agent raised his voice like a carnival barker from out of the entrance doors. "Street name A-M, to the left! Street name N-Z to the right!"

The people in front of me shuffled in what appeared to be a reluctant march, their conversations muted in a single gray hum. As I dragged myself forward in the line, Sophie visited once again. This time she appeared not as Julia, but as myself. A terrible dread expanded as I neared the front of the line. Somehow I'd be forced to choose between an old order of the traditional and a new order of the unharnessed. I didn't know who represented what. None of it felt trustworthy.

In that moment, I felt a world's suffering in the form of hot flames rising in the center of my chest. When I reached the polling cubicle inside, I stared at the computer card in a blur. After picking up the black pen, I stood paralyzed, not knowing what to do. After what seemed an awfully long time, the only thing that was there rose up.

You mean to tell me you threw away your vote? In THIS election?

I imagined the scorn from anyone I might dare tell about my choice that was emanating irresistibly from me.

What I did was write L-O-V-E on the ticket, then quickly deposited it into the machine nearby. It swallowed my ballot with an eager appetite. I almost paused, wondering if it might spit back my truth, not fitting the sorting menu of the Great Machine. I also knew the machine I was fighting against lived in my own brain. Walking across the parking lot, any peace I could've felt around that choice was overshadowed by internal condemnation. It was as if I'd just agreed with the universe to unleash the force of a fiery hell.

When I arrived at my car, I was overcome with emotion I didn't understand. I cried on and off for several hours. It seemed as if something had irrevocably changed in me and the world. I had no idea what it was. It was a massive grave of unknown grief, a holocaust of feeling. Two things were certain and they didn't feel reconcilable. Something in me at the polling station picked up the pen and knew *exactly* where to fix my gaze. But in order to get there, it seemed a shattering would happen. And I didn't want the kind of shattering I imagined to be necessary. Though reluctant, my pen called it into being. For the remainder of the day, I released from a deep well of sorrow.

I didn't understand any of it until the returns came in, watching the incredulous expressions of those who reported the breaking news. The crying ceased and was replaced with cruel relief. I now understood what had bounced up from the dark cellar of my consciousness since casting my vote. I was carrying something much larger than a personal angst. I knew our country was about to be pulled in the same painful directions Julia's arms were a week earlier. I could barely remember the heart that popped forward or the L-O-V-E I scratched on my ballot in a sense of trust.

So I totally understood what was present for Chris in the room ten days after the election as his foot circled the sphere, a huge dark shadow looming over him. I was still in the thick of feelings myself.

"Chris, what impulse is present?"

"I want to *smash* this," he replied, with a sharp and palpable honesty.

The room was silent for a moment before other voices began to stir in response.

"Smash the fucking thing. Do it," a woman in the circle across from Chris announced as she stood to add her whole body's vote into the mix.

"You can't, Chris. It's beautiful and it doesn't belong to you," a softer voice added from another part of the room.

Spoken and unspoken, many reactions played in the space of the room. We were in the midst of our own kind of haphazard electoral process. How could we reconcile the truth of the feelings of smash and shatter with the desire to keep the beauty of the bubble as it was? We'd become a living paradox.

But I knew in that moment that the bubble had already burst. We were all just catching up in some kind of reality time lag. The harsh beauty of it was this: We were now in contact with the usually buried stories about having been shattered or wanting to shatter something.

I needed to somehow create an experience for the group to honor the impulse. We needed to do it not from the "or" of judgment, which breeds further separation, but to find a way to reach for the "and" of love. We were another kind of concentration camp needing liberation. We needed air from our own self-constructed gas chamber that was holding us lifeless.

"Grab your jackets. We're going outside to get some air," I announced after all the voices, silent and spoken, had rippled through the room. I lifted the bubble-sphere out from beneath Chris's foot and asked one of the participants, a midwife, to carry it outside wrapped in the large Andean textile at the foot of her chair.

Our venue was an interfaith retreat center, an old mansion on the Connecticut coastline donated by the WT Grant estate to the Sisters of Mercy. A wooden gazebo overlooked the water a short walk outside the back door of our classroom. As we gathered inside the gazebo, I scanned for where to have the midwife gently place the wrapped sphere on the concrete floor. I imagined that the peacock-feather eyes inside exhibited a curious expression, wondering what would happen next.

Following the instinct that arose on the walk to the gazebo, I cued "Hava Nagila," the Jewish wedding song, on You Tube on my phone and handed it to my assistant. I looked up to gather the group in the field of my vision.

"Chris, since you're holding this story for all of us, are you willing to step forward to break the glass?" His movement toward me was his reply.

"While there may be other ways to do this, there's only one circumstance I can think of right now where we can take the essence of all we've been feeling about shattering and being shattered and connect it to love instead of a kind of holocaust. We want to try it on as a sacred choice and create consequence with a *Holy* Cost." I paused for a moment, as people began to realize that the gazebo had suddenly been converted into a *chuppah*, the canopy in a Jewish wedding ceremony. Playful magic was suddenly in the air.

"Chris, I think you'll need a partner for this. It's wise not to go it alone," I said with a half wink. Chris turned to Sara and invited her to step up beside him.

"Of course, we're all your partners, too. So tell me, are you willing to join your impulse to shatter, on our collective behalf, in the name of love?"

"I am!" He smiled wide. It was a loaded response.

"We are," rose out in echo from somewhere in the circle.

Chris raised his knee and dropped the sole of his boot, flattening the fragile glass sphere with a loud pop, recreating the moment in which a glass is shattered by the groom as a part of a Jewish wedding. It sounded exactly like the release of a champagne cork. Without the need to cue my assistant, "Hava Nagila" echoed out from the cell phone, which now sat on the sill of the gazebo. The group circled and did an impromptu *hora* around Chris and Sara and me. The midwife stepped forward to fold the layers of cloth over the shattered pieces. She handed it to Chris, who held it like a baby.

After a few more minutes of dance and revelry, we paused for a twenty-minute break. As the others scattered in various directions to soak in a little sun on the unusually warm November day, I wandered up the hill from the gazebo, faced the ocean, and went deep into the recesses of my heart.

None of my actions were meant to diminish the feelings present in pain. Pain can be a loving and powerful provocateur when it isn't connected to victimization and blame. And pain's opposite, pleasure, has its own set of traps. It can lead to a heavenly somewhere else unanchored to the earthly. It can take us away from the beauty of the mortal experience and its own expression of infinite and embodied wisdom. True liberation means spanning both. As George Harrison is famous for saying, "Any road will take you there." The role of the heart is to accept and flow with where the road takes us—which is always both: away, and in return.

Before I turned my back to the ocean and walked the distance to the classroom, I thought of Julia. Her courage, trust, and love would naturally lead her, her son, and his father into a new cycle of experience. The same was true for Chris, Sara, and all of us in the workshop. The same was true for a divided America that was crying out in pain and trading blame across boundary lines of red and blue.

None of us ever knows what's ahead, what will germinate naturally out of a shattering or dissolving. At best, we might have ideas about what's quietly forming inside mysterious bundles of joy, like the one folded and tucked by the midwife in the gazebo. It would hold the pieces of the sphere as seeds until something fertilized in the ground of love, ready to open into the light of a new day.

I laughed to myself as I approached the back door to the retreat center, imagining the peacock's midnight-blue eyes focused together in a gaze of that love, courtesy of the necessary shattering.

Chris was right. The whole world *was* burning. Following his lead, we were stepping into the magic of the spheres. And it was hot with the fire and passion of love.

Chapter 21

Accept the Winds of Change

If I were a mirror
I'd be one so to serve you.
Even the harshest image
travels inward more gently
in softer light.

And though I couldn't control
the shade or bright around me,
if I let myself soften with age;
if I accepted the scratches and blurs
in the silver living behind my glass front
as a biography of all the times
I was knocked around, moved roughly,
put in places I didn't belong...

maybe some of the impenetrable smoothness
of perfect reflection could open up.

~ Robert Cole, excerpted from "Luminous"

એ

"I hardly ever think about the tornado anymore, it was so long ago," my childhood friend Christine said when I called to talk with her about the storm that leveled her house nearly thirty years before.

"The timing of your call is really weird, Pat. The whole thing came up out of nowhere last week. I was walking through the furniture store down by Long Wharf and I saw this makeup mirror. It was just like the one I sat at as a kid. It stopped me dead in my tracks; I actually froze when I saw it. It's the thing I lost in the tornado that I miss the most."

Christine was the class troublemaker in seventh grade. She was rough and gruff, always spoiling for some kind of fight. We were unlikely friends. I was the bookish nerd who sat behind her and kept to myself in a new school where smart wasn't considered very cool. She tortured and loved me. Torment was not only her initiation, but one of the ways her big heart drew me into her web, along with a host of others, where she's kept us ever since. Despite remaining about as opposite as two people could be, friendship endured.

The September I met Christine was a tender time for me. As if simply being twelve years old wasn't enough vulnerability for a lifetime, over the course of one summer, I had to face leaving a school and friends I loved in Massachusetts to move with my family to New Hampshire. My parents bought a picturesque house in a charming neighborhood in half hope of saving their marriage after my father left his high-level job in favor of a less stressful one.

My sister and I were promised fall foliage, crackling fireplace fires, and snowmobile rides down logging roads.

When the plan for an idyllic reset failed during the fiery August that followed, my sister returned to college and I moved with my mother to Connecticut just two weeks before the start of seventh grade. I was shattered from being shuttled across two state lines in two months, right in the midst of a more difficult border crossing called early adolescence.

Christine and I were also mirrors, seeing in each other something that lived tucked away in each of our shadows. I was fragile and needed a tough friend. She needed to put me on a pedestal she had trouble climbing on her own. A lifelong match was made from sporadic arguments followed by long periods of silence, a mutual love for writing dramatic pre-teen poetry, and a shared spiritual connection she continues to deny, or at least downplay, to this day.

This was the foundation that allowed Christine to come out to me at almost thirteen, when coming out wasn't even a catch phrase yet.

She was popular with everyone, maybe because her toughness was a little fearsome or everyone spied the same enormous heart I did beneath her poorly hidden bully exterior. Or both. Or other reasons entirely. But she held some kind of command over two highly polished floors lined in yellow lockers at a small Catholic junior high staffed by the Sisters of the Sacred Heart—patrolling the halls like the cop her older sister later became.

Some of her toughness came from the streets. When Christine was very young, her mother divorced. She and her two sisters, all two years apart, spent lots of time in Brooklyn in the apartment of her Italian grandmother, while her mother worked.

Her Aunt Marie lived in the same building at the other end of the hall. Ent-Re, as she was known in the family, was also her godmother. On the days when looking after three little girls was too much for her grandmother, Ent-Re watched Christine. Pumped by being chosen for special private time, Christine ran down the hall from her grandmother's front door to slide in her socks onto the marble floor of Ent Re's apartment.

The white makeup vanity, or makeup mirror as Christine referred to it, sat in Ent-Re's bedroom. Ent-Re was a beautician. When Christine behaved, she was rewarded with a seat at this home salon. The promise of the makeup mirror was the one thing that mattered most to Christine, which seemed funny, since she wasn't at all the makeup-wearing type. Twenty years later, the same piece of furniture stood proudly in the bedroom of Christine's first home—until the remains of the house appeared on the front page of the *New York Post* in July 1989 when a rogue summer thunderstorm spawned a tornado in Connecticut and reduced everything she owned to rubble.

"The makeup mirror Ent-Re gave me ... do you remember it from when I lived at the Dudley Street house?" That's one of the great things about a long friendship; you can mark the passage of time in terms of former street addresses.

"It was really incredible," Christine continued. "The one I saw in the furniture store was white, like that one was. Except mine didn't have three mirrors, it had four. Two of them folded from the sides to the center like most do, but this makeup table had a mirror top, so you could look down and see yourself. So why the hell are you calling to ask me about the tornado?" I heard the same bully tone in her voice that was her hallmark for more than forty years.

To Christine, I was her "kooky" bohemian friend. She still put me on a pedestal, despite the fact that I lived at the edge of a place she preferred to avoid, such as my attempts at conversation about the church she was mad at for not accepting who she was and whom she loved, cordoned off like the police tape that surrounded her former house before it was bulldozed. "Well, I'm writing a book connected to my work. The theme is sort of about accepting things as they are and finding value in difficult situations. Naturally, I thought of you and the tornado."

"So, basically, you're calling to ask me about what good came out of the tornado? Well, that's easy. Nothing. Not a thing. Only loss. It's hard to explain. Unless it happens to you, you can't understand. No one can. Since I was visiting my grandmother in New York when it happened, I at least had my car and a suitcase and a couple of changes of clothes and even a little jewelry. But my sister Laurie, who'd just gone out an hour before the storm in her friend's car, had only a pair of flip-flops, a tank top, and a pair of shorts. You remember, right? She was living upstairs from me at the time."

I did remember. I also remembered how Christine's oldest sister Linda was on police patrol during the storm and the horror she encountered at being called to one of the homes in town that collapsed when the tornado hit. Not only was it the two-family house of her younger siblings, Laurie's car was underneath the rubble and Linda thought it meant she was inside. Broken gas lines made approaching the house impossible. Linda stood at the side of the road in her blues, weeping for the sister she thought was gone. Then she had to radio their stepfather, who was also the chief of police, about what she'd discovered.

"I still get emotional when I think about what Linda and my dad went through." Christine's voice cracked and rose through the phone. "I was spared from all of it. I was in New York, and they hadn't called me yet."

"I can't imagine what that was like," I replied quietly, recognizing Christine was crying softly on the other end of the phone. Christine's mother also went through temporary hell; it wasn't until Laurie called her when she arrived in her neighborhood to find the roads cut off that anyone knew she was still alive.

"And you know what was really awful? Losing photos. My entire personal history—erased. Worse even than that was the tweezers. I've never found a pair of tweezers since that were like the ones I lost in the tornado. Isn't that a crazy thing to focus on? But the makeup mirror? That was freakin' devastating."

Later, because of the fear of gas lines rupturing, she and her sister weren't allowed to retrieve a single item from the heap that was a mix of her house and its contents. They could only watch from afar while the steel teeth of hungry machines bulldozed and carried it all away. The landfill wouldn't even let them in to try to scavenge what they could. They not only lost everything, they could see everything right in front of them and had no ability to recover an ounce of it.

After listing all the true horrors of the experience, I didn't even have to bring her back to my original question before she began enumerating all the things that occurred that weren't losses, but gains. They followed naturally after getting the story about "nothing good about it" out of the way.

"You know, come to think of it now, being forced to move in with my mother and stepfather was a great thing for me and them. I was around to give them a hand, especially as they got older, in ways I wouldn't have otherwise. I never would have gotten the job I had at Colony, which led me to get my MBA. In fact, I guess I wouldn't even be living where I am right now if the tornado hadn't happened," she concluded, without a word in edgewise from me and as if she was considering for the first time that it did, after all, have some value.

Christine loved the home she currently owned. She took a level of pride in it that was obvious to everyone, especially her neighbors. In fact, a few of the men in the neighborhood petitioned her to stop making so many improvements around her house, complaining that she was showing them up and their wives were after them to get busy. This was one of the things Christine was known for—the non-stop process of beautifying where she lived.

But before I had a chance to say a word about the richness I heard in her monologue, Christine called an abrupt halt to our conversation. "Look, my friend has been waiting for me this whole time. We were watching a movie. I really gotta go, Pat. I don't know if any of this is what you were looking for, but call me this week and we can talk more if you need to. I have a project going on, planting bushes outside the house, but I'll make the time for you."

"Wait just a minute," I replied, sniffing a storm in the air behind her words. "What do you mean you're planting bushes during the week? Are you telecommuting five days now or are you on vacation?" There was a short pause on the other end of the phone. Something was sitting in the silence.

"I can't go into it right now," she said in a hushed voice that raised my worry.

"Uh-uh. No way. That's not fair," I said, being pushy in a way you only could with a childhood friend. "Movie or not, give me the really short version. What's going on?"

Christine's voice dropped even more. All the energy and excitement it held from the gratitude had drained out. "I lost my job. The company downsized and a bunch of us were laid off. I got a few months' severance, but I don't know what I'm gonna do. Who's gonna hire me at the pay grade I'm at now?" I knew Christine was making six figures. "My house payment is dependent on that salary. Look, really I gotta go, we'll talk later," she said, then hung up.

As I disconnected our call, a storm of images hit.

More than thirty years later, unexpected change threatened to take away Christine's house a second time. What were the chances of that?

And what were her choices?

For one, she could hide in the basement in fear, generating resumés for similar jobs, while the twisting winds of unemployment threatened outside.

For another, she could pine for the loss of her job and wish for its perfect replacement, like the tweezers that gave her the ability to control the tiniest details of things, plucking them out one at a time rather than succumbing to the quicker pass of accepting a massive loss of everything all at once.

Or rather than being haunted by fate as an enemy, she could use the makeup mirror to see her own powerful capacity to withstand destruction until it brings about renewal. She could be bolstered, rather than diminished, by her past experience, and have trust in this new one. All it would take would be for her to remember.

Christine wasn't my client. She was my old friend, whom I spoke to only a handful of times a year, even though she lived not too far away. She didn't even really understand what I did for a living. Maybe I could stop by while she planted bushes this week and help her recall what she already knew better than anyone.

The total loss that brings us to the tomb is also the womb. Christine was already a master at accepting the winds of change. The tornado gave her no choice. She just needed the makeup mirror to remember and reflect that mastery.

Chapter 22

Open to the Unthinkable

I am releasing the prisoners,
one by one.
The cells opening,
bars giving way;
light in the courtyard saying
come out
with your heads up.
All is forgiven.
Only take the door, please,
and my pardons
long-delayed
for original sins
never truly committed.

~ Robert Cole, "Releasing the Prisoners"

ço

When I got the news that Caron was on suicide watch at Garner Correctional Facility, I couldn't stop crying.

I was plagued by thoughts that conjured him sitting at the edge of some anonymous cold steel bed, crouched over with his head in hands, pulling desperately at the short edges of his close-cropped dark hair. It was a posture I knew well. I saw it occasionally when we met at my office for sessions, where the outer expression of his internal struggle was evident, a battle with an enemy that was invisible to both of us, but present nonetheless.

The lawyer hired for him by his family—the only person able to see him so far—shared that Caron reported no recollection of the incident that occurred a few days before, when he attacked his mother with a knife while she slept beside his dad in their bed in the dark of the night.

It was nearly unbearable for me to imagine how he might feel if the memory returned, when he fully realized the impact of his actions on the family I knew he loved so deeply. Whether he'd remembered yet or not, I had no way of knowing.

I got to know Caron over a span of about six years: from the young teenager caught in the grip of substance abuse, then an older teen making his way through a maze of self-discovery, sobriety, and recovery, to a young man experiencing the onset of the diagnosis called schizophrenia.

Caron was a gifted rapper, a poet who could scratch lyrics on a scrap of paper in a few short minutes while using his bent knee as a table. His hip-hop verse cut to the core of things with keen observation and a surgical precision. I knew Caron carried tremendous insight, even if it was sometimes covered in a thick veil of confusion. He had an enormous heart.

I wondered who would believe that now.

I became even more upset imagining a world poised to misconstrue the whole of who I knew him to be, a world that might judge him only on the brutal reality of this one incorrigible action. I wasn't crying out of a desire to rescue or shield him from responsibility. I was enormously saddened by the fact that his life might come to be singly identified by what happened in the midst of one dark unconscious night.

I knew it would be difficult for many people to reconcile the young man I knew with the individual indicted for attempted murder in a middle-class suburban neighborhood.

After hearing the news, I dug into a packed-away box to recover something that Caron wrote. The first line kept circling in my head: *I got mad heart.* I wanted to read the rest to see if it might offer some clue about this insane occurrence or maybe provide some small comfort.

I finally found what I was looking for. A picture of a sleek black jaguar looked out from behind the clear plastic cover of a binder. Inside the front pocket was the folded piece of loose-leaf paper he scratched on nearly two years before.

I got mad heart
And try to leave behind the drama the past starts
Grasp stars ...
More tracks than a Nascar rap-jaguar at large.
Sometime you gotta leave behind what's chained up,
But I'll raise the volume until that sleeping giant wakes up.
A lethal mind redesigns when demons try to break us.
Hard headed like Easter Island people,
It's my make up
But change is up.

He'd raised the volume, all right. It was easy, in retrospect, to see the lethal mind was there a couple of years earlier, though none of us knew about the impulse. I sensed Caron had been trying to combat the demons for a long time before the night they won out.

The couple of years that followed the rap he wrote was a mix of progress and setback for him, but mostly progress. Fewer were the times when he stared off into space and seemed to slip between some crack into another world and more when he was fully lucid, conversant, and grounded. He was gratified with starting a job that gave him purpose, pleased with the verses we wrote together as he and I explored his talent and the creative contributions he could bring to the world.

He'd recently taken on a facilitator role at a local Narcotics Anonymous meeting and couldn't wait to tell me how excited he was that he'd connected with a sponsor to lead him in working each of the twelve steps.

The last time I spoke to Caron was only a few weeks back, just after his twenty-first birthday and ten days before the life-changing incident that no one saw coming. He called that day to cancel our appointment. He told me he felt anxiety building and planned to go to the psychiatric unit at the local hospital. It was a self-regulating and insightful decision that came from him, rather than from the concerns of others around him, as it had in the past.

Just over a week later, he was released from that hospital stay. The staff expressed confidence he was doing okay. Later that night, the surprising attack changed everything irrevocably.

I visited his mom, Leah, in the ICU the day after her emergency admission to the hospital. Despite a puncture wound that came close to the edge of her brain and another that missed her heart by less than an inch, plus needing surgery on both hands and a hundred fifty stiches to her head and face, she was strong and alert. It was a miracle she was alive. She was surrounded by family that loved her, the same family that loved Caron still.

I watched her twelve-year-old son slip on a pair of latex gloves while dressed in a pair of scrubs he mischievously swiped from a nearby supply closet. He sat down at her bedside and lovingly stroked her exposed forearm while he fixed his gaze down on the big gauze mitts that covered her hands like a pair of white boxing gloves.

Leah had been in the ring of battle for sure, but emerged uncannily fine, given what had happened. She told me she remembered only waking up with a start in the middle of the night and found herself shouting "NO!" With her hands, she pushed Caron away as he loomed over their bed with a knife taken from its home in a wooden sleeve in their gourmet kitchen.

A half-hour later, I watched another member of the family, Caron's younger sister, jump up to assist an aide as she prepared to move her mom across the hall to the surgical wing. Leah was now free from the leash of the IV and no longer needed the necessary watch of intensive care.

I knew Caron's mom's history. She, too, had been a client, plus a student in one of my programs. She grew up in Manhattan, raised in privilege by a family of philanthropists. I knew she almost lost her own mother to a brain tumor when she was a young girl, not too different in age from the daughter who now matched her careful steps as she walked to a new hospital room across the hall. I knew she'd lived with two half-siblings who had schizophrenia and I was familiar with the impact of that story on her life.

Like all of nature, history often repeats itself in a series of shorter and longer cycles, but never in the exact same way. I also realized it was possible that the same cycle could shift precipitously in another go-round, a great evolution in a single revolution. Even within one lifetime.

When Caron appeared to go missing in the dark neural passageways of his brain, it was my sense that his mother appeared for him as a kind of external genetic marker or a target for something that lived in him he could neither identify nor get a handle on. This all-encompassing experience seemed to extend, by his own admission, to the way he characterized his relationship to addiction as a seductive feminine force he couldn't get away from.

I wondered if he knew, if only unconsciously, that what was happening inside him was stealing the usual pleasures and pain of growing up in the way his siblings and peers experienced. He probably got a hint, at least, when he was pulled out of the local public school at fifteen to attend an inpatient substance-abuse program out west.

Now nearing adulthood, when developmentally he was supposed to be leaving to explore life on his own, seeing and hearing his mother provoked a strong desire to separate that he couldn't actualize. At least, that was my two-bit pseudo diagnosis from a purely non-clinical, instinctive view.

When I arrived at their home to drop off food for the family the morning after seeing Leah at the hospital, Tango, the perfectly named family dog, greeted me with the usual cheer and wagging tail when Caron's dad, Arthur, opened the door. It was if Tango didn't know or couldn't recall what had gone on just two nights before. She'd already shaken it off somehow. *Lucky are the animals*, I thought.

I handed Caron's dad the bag I carried in from Whole Foods and asked, "How's she doing?"

"Pretty good this morning. They've got her well drugged for the pain. But she's asking a lot of questions now, especially about Caron. She wanted to know if I knew where he'd been taken. But I have no idea where he is," Arthur said as he passed off the grocery bundle to one of the older boys who came from another direction to answer my knock at the door. "Come on upstairs. Let me show you where it happened."

I followed him up the steps to their second-floor bedroom. The bed was already gone. It had broken in half, Arthur explained, when he stood on it and leapt to tackle his son. An exposed subfloor revealed the area where men dressed in protective gear had ripped up the bloody rug the previous morning.

"Well, we'd just discussed getting rid of the carpet to put in a hardwood floor," he nervously joked, fighting his own waves of traumatic memory with whatever gallows humor he could muster.

"You know, it's so weird. Leah, probably only a week ago, talked about wanting to back off on taking clients for her massage therapy practice. She was saying her hands needed a break." He paused, then added, "I hope the surgery goes okay." The worry he carried was etched all over his face.

"You know what's most bizarre? I sharpened the kitchen knives the very morning Caron returned from the hospital. I do it fairly often, cuz we hate using knives that don't cut well. And then when the surgeon came in to evaluate Leah, he told us that if the knife Caron used hadn't been as sharp as it was, the cuts to her thumbs could have resulted in irreparable damage. The whole thing is just so unbelievable," Arthur said, as he pointed to the corner of the room. "It happened over there."

As I listened to his story, it appeared to me as if circumstances on some level carried a knowing of what was about to unfold and, unconsciously, everyone prepared for their part.

As I looked around this ordinary master bedroom that had become a crime scene, it was hard to shake the feeling that something more than a subfloor had been exposed beneath the rug. When Caron's dad picked up a photo resting on his wife's bureau of Caron as a young child, grinning wide alongside his two toddler-aged brothers, I knew what it was. It wasn't anguish, anger, fear, or trauma.

It was love, and it was present as a stronger force than the violence that had been unleashed in this room.

Arthur turned to me and made a very personal admission.

"Pat, I can tell *you* this. I had Caron's head locked in my arm. I could've killed him ... my own son. I didn't think that at the time. I wasn't thinking anything. I just jumped from the bed on top of him and took him down. But I've had thoughts since then that I could've ended it right then ... for him, and for us."

With a truly agonized expression, Arthur turned away from me to look at the photo that was framed on Leah's dresser. "But this is my first-born son. Look at him. I could never do that."

By now, we both were crying.

A few days later, after Caron's mom successful surgery and discharge from the hospital, I visited their home again. As Leah and I walked together across the kitchen to the living room, I noticed the granite center island had turned into a garden. Get-well flower arrangements covered what used to be home to dirty dishes and open peanut-butter jars with cast-off lids. The counters were filled with platters and trays, food that had been delivered by friends and family in her absence. She told me that one of her kids' bus drivers, whom she didn't know by more than a wave, came by after her school run to drop off two bags of groceries for the family.

The house at the end of their cul-de-sac had even become a magnet for strangers' love.

As we passed through the kitchen, Leah turned to me with a wide grin. "Arthur says the real town news headlines should've read: "Wife hospitalized after murder attempt, husband gains twenty pounds."

It was clear to me, after being in the house for less than a few minutes, that humor, annoyance, the rush of who needed to go where, and the squabbles of four other siblings in the background evidenced a somewhat restored routine in this close-knit family. Yet according to Leah, during quiet pauses, one or another of the children would come over unprompted and curl up in her arms. Her still-bandaged hands assured that no one could really forget what had happened a little more than a week before.

When we arrived in the living room to sit together on the couch, I half expected her to tell me she wasn't sleeping so well back in her home. So it was a surprise when Leah leaned forward and dropped her voice as if hiding from secret listeners in the room.

"Pat, I get it. I do. *This was an initiation.*" There was utter clarity in her voice. Having been one of my students, Leah understood that difficult passages were often catalysts of new cycles of life.

She then proceeded to tell me how she fully understood that the incident with Caron was meant to bring her
to more alertness. It was an urgent call for her to awaken,
figuratively and literally, from a deep sleep.

But I'll raise the volume until that sleeping giant wakes up.
Caron's words from the rap played in my head as she spoke.

From my seat on this comfortable beige sectional in
this beautiful home in the middle of suburbia, I studied
Caron's mom's stitched up face and watched it distort
slightly as the impact of her words landed with me. The
room wobbled. My gaze moved beyond her to a mirror that
hung over the fireplace.

Just like Alice in *Through the Looking Glass,* some part
of me escaped the room and stepped through the mirror to
enter another world, this one a dense jungle of feeling.

From a distance, I could hear her fading voice say, "He
opened my vision so I could see what I need to step into in
my own life's work … My head, my heart, it was the *only*
way it could've happened. I was resisting looking at and
feeling so much."

My heart was pounding in my temples and every cell
of my being screamed internally. *It. Is. Way. Too. Early. For.
This.* The only thing that existed for me in that moment on
the other side of the mirrored glass was my own volcanic
echo of the "NO!" she shouted when Caron loomed over
her that night.

Yes, Leah had taken on exactly what I largely practice
and offer others with my work: If we remain present to
what is as it is, greet it as an expression of something of great
value beyond the changing reactions and responses of the
mind and emotions, some imaginable form of beauty and
wholeness reveals itself.

But right now, as I sat in a proverbial ring of fire with a woman who looked like a prizefighting warrior with those white boxing-glove hands, I wanted to push back with a level of resistance not unlike her own, upstairs at three in the morning a week earlier.

She's dissociating, I thought, as the onslaught in my head continued. *This is horrible. It wasn't supposed to happen this way—for her, for Caron, for anybody.* I was lost in a tantrum of feeling, in spite of the fact that I simultaneously understood that this had been, in fact, an initiatory experience.

I've heard it said in many circles that when a great awakening occurs, the awakened should be ready for an even greater pushback. Whether that was true or not, I didn't know. But it would explain what came next: The worst voice of all emerged as I sat in witness to the love that Leah was bringing to the unthinkable, as if I, too, had received an initiating cut to my own forehead.

Those so-called wisdom teachings you shared with her in your role as teacher and coach? Not only are they taking her away from this reality, they caused her to ignore cues around her that could have saved Caron from being on suicide watch behind bars and could have cost her own life. YOU are personally responsible.

Over the denunciation of cause and effect playing out inside me, Leah's voice surfaced outside of me once again. I had no idea what else she added before I was brought back closer to the room again.

"I want you to tell this story in the book you're writing. I want it to help other people wake up, to realize that amazing opportunities are available in terrible things that happen." She said this with absolute clarity.

Yeah, right, I thought through the mirrored glass that created a safe distance between us.

It felt like the kind of thick glass partition that distorted voices and separated prisoners from their visitors in TV dramas. It took everything I could muster in that moment to exit backwards through the looking glass and once again be fully in the room.

The inner protest softened, but didn't disappear as I tried to stay present enough to listen while she went on excitedly, almost giddy, to tell me what happened during her discharge from the hospital.

"Pat, you won't believe this. When Arthur went to pull up the car, a young orderly came to get me in a wheelchair. He wheeled it over to me and said, 'Hi, I'm Caron. I've come to take you home.' What are the chances of *that* happening? Caron's such an unusual name," Leah said with a wave of excitement in her voice. We both knew what she read in that occurrence. Home is where the heart is, the hearth is, the love is. It was a metaphor of great comfort.

She continued to share the other discoveries and links she made as she lay recovering in her hospital bed, having been opened by an experience that would have sent most people into terror, rage, regret, or self-pity.

Leah spoke about her vulnerability and what it was like to experience the physical limitations from her injuries; how she had to lean on her husband in a way that she'd been saying she wanted to for years, but had resisted.

She talked about her other children's reactions and the healing shifts occurring for them, and she told me again how she felt called to share with the larger world that when something painful and terrible happens, it doesn't have to live forever as a story of trauma.

Leah reported that on the night she came home from the hospital, she went over to the yoga studio where she taught to reassure her students that she was okay and that they shouldn't worry.

Meanwhile, I wanted to reach way up, grab her feet, pull her back down to Earth, and insist that she look at the reality in front of *me*, the one where something unspeakably awful had occurred. In that moment, while I understood her perspective more than most would, having given myself over to the practice of all-things-are-holy, I was simultaneously recording this place of feeling as the resoundingly louder reality.

For the first time in eleven years of this work, I found myself experiencing the kind of fierce judgment and stubborn resistance with which my clients sometimes arrived at my office. It wasn't that Leah had turned the tables on my reflexive way of engaging the world. That would assume one right way and one wrong way to be with what confronts us at opposite ends of the table. The tables weren't turning *on* me; I wasn't dumped on my metaphorical head as a victim. Rather, I was initiated into a deeper level of empathy for feelings as holy harbingers themselves.

I managed to finish our visit in a dutiful, supportive way while much continued to stir inside me. And as I got up to hug Leah goodbye, the emotions began to loosen a little of their grip. I'd been with them one hundred percent, enough for me to realize that *it took something this big to shake me.* Ninety-nine percent wouldn't have done it. I needed to go all the way to the far end of the dial.

I'll raise the volume until that sleeping giant wakes up. I heard Caron's words again and knew they were also for me. He'd initiated so many of us into the gift of staying present to the divine undesired and holy unthinkable.

After leaving the family's home, I drove twenty minutes to my own, allowing the thoughts to reel through my mind without resisting.

I recalled a news event I witnessed some time earlier during floods in the Midwest. In one town, the river rose so high that many residents had to be evacuated to local shelters. An interviewer was reporting live from a shelter where townspeople were taken.

"We heard you were taken by boat from your home yesterday. Could you tell us what that was like?" The reporter raised the mic to catch an elderly woman's reply.

She lit up. "It was *so* much fun. I've never been in a big raft like *that* before. It was really something."

The reporter, clearly uneasy or disappointed at not having found some deeper and more newsworthy trauma, tried again with the tiniest hint of a whine in her newscaster voice. "But didn't you have to leave behind all of your belongings?"

The old woman countered, "Yes, but it's dry here and the food is very, very good."

The reporter quickly moved on in search of victims of the flood who were actually traumatized. She obviously couldn't deal with someone in dire circumstances present enough to accept what is as it is and shake it off with the same ease as Tango the dog did with her tail at Caron's house.

Thoughts like this continued to pass as I drove, and I realized this event exposed a place I hadn't confronted directly in my own life, a life that was largely blessed and populated, to date anyway, with mere garden-variety pain and trauma. But here I was, introduced to a new level of feeling. I had a choice as to how I held what was there, as would others. What would Caron and his whole family do with their feelings as more time passed between that night and the unfolding future? What about the judge's feelings, the jury's feelings, the psychiatrists representing the defendant and the prosecution's feelings about this? Would they be able to see this occurrence in any kind of holy way? Leah would guide us even as she might have to confront her own waves of feeling rising on the tide of the future. We were all here to help one another remember.

By the time I arrived at my house, I was exhausted—emotionally, mentally, and physically.

I stepped out of the car and walked the path to my front door. As I approached, I looked over to the laughing Buddha that stood guard on our front lawn.

Without thinking, a few days earlier, I'd placed a set of oversized keys on a ring into one of the hands of that jolly statue. They were a gift from a colleague. She told me at the time that she didn't know why, but she was certain when she saw the faux-rusty keys on the shelf at a local gift store that they were for me.

As I walked past, I suddenly saw him as the laughing warden Buddha. And in that moment, I accepted my own initiation from Caron. The invitation he'd presented to me was to come home and be imprisoned with both the bigger-picture presence of beauty in all things and powerful expressions of raw emotion. I was invited to recognize that being fully alive meant spanning the full spectrum of both. The field beyond right-doing and wrong-doing that Rumi spoke of in his famous poem was no more sacred than the ideas of wrong-doing and right-doing themselves. All perspectives share holy ground. These polarities belonged together.

I smiled when I *saw* that the Buddha had a wink to his eye. As I passed him by to approach the front door, I heard him whisper something softly to me.

"Hello, my name is Caron. I'm here to welcome you home."

The warden Buddha's keys jingled in the cold February air, marking, with ritual sound, another new beginning.

Chapter 23

Lie on Her

Not a single one of us could ever come close to understanding what the Cherokee Red Fire Priest had been through in Vietnam. Yet neither sympathy nor empathy was what he truly needed, as they acted as a kind of germ, an infectious agent that allowed the larger lie the Red Fire Priest told to continue to propagate in his life and ours.

All of us present on this hotter-than-usual late October day in the Arizona desert were also liars in our own right.

The sun shone with a fierce intensity. Thirty of us from across the U.S. and as far away as Canada and Australia gathered to camp on sacred land in the mountains above Tucson. Our site was an ancient caldera, a volcano that had blown millennia ago, moving the tops of nearby mountains to form the seven mounds of earth that surrounded us now.

The Red Fire Priest, steward of this land, referred to it as the Valley of the Seven Sisters.

We were called there from paved deserts far away—a mix of black, red, and white, young and old. Those of us sporting pale faces wore sunscreen as thick as war paint.

We came to circle around the fire one by one to tell our stories, to reveal to ourselves and one another where we felt bound by our various forms of untruth. We were there to allow the wisdom of being caught in lies to keep us captive long enough to receive the *medicine* contained within the stories themselves that we couldn't see without the gifts the others presented to us.

We sat on chairs and benches beneath a wooden structure that the Red Fire Priest said was a medicine wheel. It was shaped like a star tetrahedron, the Cherokee Star. It loomed overhead and provided striations of relief from the sun in the form of narrow, angular shade. The Red Fire Cherokee flag flew over this stark, austere spot, sporting an apt symbol for this arid place, the fire-breathing dragon. Next to it, another medicine flag flapped in the wind, one with an eagle, condor, panther, and tiger, beautifully painted beneath the sparkle of the seven brightest stars of the Pleiades cluster.

One of the first to step forward to the fire was an Aztec man who challenged those in the circle who wore hats and sunglasses to take them off. "Stop your hiding," he said in the harsh tone of a cranky grandfather. It was hard to determine if it was meant as a heartfelt invitation to connect or a critical request of those who feared frying in the sun.

A lean muscled black man from Harlem responded to the challenge in a unique and immediate way. He stood up and slowly walked over to the red man. In silence, he removed not only his sunglasses and hat, but also his belt, shorts, and underwear, then returned naked to his chair in the circle for the remainder of the day.

The meeting immediately shifted into a sort of high-stakes medicine-wheel-of-fortune unlike any kind found in the Las Vegas desert to the north. It was a gamble of the highest order, as to cease hiding or lying was to risk vulnerability, a figurative nakedness embodied by the man who disrobed in our midst, in the hopes of acquiring some other form of riches yet to be determined.

Next to rise was the strong and beautiful fifty-something white woman who was a national expert on wolves and had been born with cerebral palsy. She approached the fire supported by two metal crutches under her arms. As she neared the center, she began to cry, expressing through choking sobs the feeling of drowning in her own shame.

She recounted the story of parents who, out of enormous love for their daughter, protected and shielded her from her physical difference by taking every opportunity to remind her that she was *just like everybody else.*

The sting of how that lived within her as a lie let loose a torrent of tears. It was a desert mirage that appeared for her and all of us, as if it were the result of a lifetime of bone-dry thirst for a hidden truth.

It seemed her sorrow was endless as she buckled over, draining a reservoir of grief, near the fire's edge.

"Bring me water," I said as I moved to stand behind her. Someone from the circle handed me the bowl and I began to pour it slowly over her head, adding to the emotional levee break in her eyes. "Don't give up, love. Trust your instinct to drown in the truth."

This time, I wanted her to go *all the way* rather than caving in or withdrawing. I hoped the wave of tears would swell into a tsunami. I intended the water to encourage her not to stop short and try to make it better, or right, or attempt to resolve the split of two competing lies: being vastly different than, as well as completely the same as, everyone around her.

It was time to open the floodgates and fill the ravine.

The more she released, the more she became one with the ocean of her own grief and shame. Her two dangling legs formed a mermaid's tail right before our eyes. The bringing together of two truths was complete. We carried her back to her chair at the edge of the circle, certain in her absolute quiet that she'd found herself swimming in the deep, like the painting of a mermaid she told us hung over her bathtub at home.

A kind of steam now rose from her place where water and heat met, giving the Red Fire Priest a spectral presence as he stepped into the circle under the medicine wheel.

Born around Christmas on a Cherokee reservation in Oklahoma, he never knew his father. Even his actual birth date was uncertain; at the time, native reservations had no formal means of documenting or recording births. Early in his childhood, his mother and grandmother told him that he'd been born at an auspicious time, which indicated that he'd be the one to remember and carry the medicine stories of the Cherokee people to future generations. By his own account, this was a call to duty that the Red Fire Priest resisted and refused as far back as he could remember.

As a young man, he received a second call to duty: a draft notice that came in the mail while still in high school. Three days after his graduation in 1968, rather than refuse or dodge, he enlisted in the military.

When I first met the Red Fire Priest more than a year earlier, he told me about his deployment to Vietnam. It was far from a tale of heroic wartime service. It was, rather, the story of an enormously angry and bitter soldier who described himself as a hired assassin by a victimizing U.S. government. He laid blame on his commanding officers for intentionally tapping the deeply rooted anger of U.S. Native peoples and cleverly and cynically organizing them to inflict the most heinous violence on villages in jungles halfway across the world, giving them the worst assignments in the war.

When I first heard his story, I encouraged the Red Fire Priest to own the assassin, to put to conscious use his sharpshooter skills and annihilate the judgment that blocked him from the love he craved and the vibrant, revitalized tribe he envisioned.

He didn't seem ready then, even metaphorically, to take up arms, to shoot the lifelessness from his story with the expertise he'd honed as a warrior. At the time, even the suggestion of being honored as a veteran was too painful to consider. In the framework of right and wrong, this saga could never heal.

I'll never forget the guttural and terrifying moan of, "No, please don't," that he had uttered one year before when each of us in turn said, "Thank you," "We honor you," "We're grateful for what you have done."

This fantastically beautiful, long-winded, dry-humored, big-hearted man was a prisoner of war held in the unconscious by an angry dragon that lived on the surface of the sand in the same way the flag on the pole above him whipped in the desert wind. I remembered it all as the Red Fire Priest stepped forward and began to address the gathered group on that October day in his slow Oklahoma drawl. The story that defined him was about to be told again. I stood inside the circle with him near the fire as he spoke, this time hearing a part of the story I hadn't before. "And I brought every man in *my* unit back alive," he said, swelling with great pride.

As I focused in on him, what I saw so clearly was the walking dead. While the Red Fire Priest may have made it physically back to the U.S. with his unit, he carried with him all the horror of his encounters in Vietnam, as well as those of his entire troop, with him. Nothing had been left behind in the jungles of Southeast Asia. Every bit of the pain, suffering, anger, and death filled his form and had organized every nihilistic step of his journey since. No release of passion, purpose, or leadership for his people could be fully possible unless his rage was laid to rest.

I walked from the center fire toward the Red Fire Priest and softly began to chant. "Liar, liar, liar."

I had no strategy in my mind, no intention, no place where I saw this going. In that moment, I was utterly empty and willing only to speak what was there to be said.

The Red Fire Priest ignored me and continued to talk over the haunting background of my words. I didn't stop, getting even closer to him.

I could hear small, hot, breathless gasps around the circle and felt enormous emotion swell around me. A backdraft of heat took the shape of these imagined words from all the directions under the seven-pointed star: *Why is she doing this? This is wrong; he's an elder. She's interrupting his story. She's taunting him. What if he explodes? Are we safe here? This is getting far too hot and possibly out of control.*

It was true. I was turning up the heat.

In turn, the Red Fire Priest raised the volume of his voice to overpower mine. I dropped my words to a whisper as I approached him, taking myself to bent knee on the ground in front of him.

"You're a liar," I repeated, emphatically, though softly, looking up into his angry eyes.

In that moment, the Red Fire Priest turned into the dragon on the high-flying flag. He shook his trembling finger down at me and bellowed in a great fire breath, "*Let! Me! Finish! I get to tell my story.*" One of the core principles of Cherokee meetings and ceremonies is that everyone gets to speak for as long as they wish. I knew I was violating the rules of engagement as a guest on this land.

I froze in knee-down position, waited for some time before rising, then turned my back and walked a distance from him, kicking sand, giving space for the angry dragon to do what it needed to do. As I did, I knew without seeing—and somehow trusted—that passion and purpose were nearer to freedom.

After a few minutes, I looked up and began again. "Liar. Liar. Liar." Then I heard it in my own repetition. My voice simply slowed it down. "Liar, liar, lie on her, lie on her, lie on her."

I circled the fire and approached him again, pointing downward. My voice softened and I motioned for others to come forward, asking without words for all of them to join the soft chant. He needed all of us with him. I reached my hand up to grab his. His voice began to break and the same low guttural moan I heard a year earlier rose up and emerged in an enormous swell of grief.

"Lie on her, lie on her. Let yourself fall, soldier."

At some point, he buckled and the others circled around him, softening his complete collapse to the ground.

Finally, the soldier, the killer, the assassin whose blood-less existence held only regret and anger and shame, could rest. He could lie on Her, great Mother Earth, who in layers of sacred sand could absorb every ghost of judgment he carried, every torment he imprisoned within himself.

In the hot afternoon, all stood still.

Chapter 24

Vanish Into the Vortex: From Bliss to Abyss

The Cherokee medicine woman turned to me as she returned the two sacred artifacts into their leather pouch. I watched as she tied the strings tightly together at the top. She placed the small bag in my hand, looked directly at me, and said, "Why don't you bring these to the others who couldn't join us? Maybe you can create a way to include them in what just happened here. The rest of us will meet you back there in a little while."

I nodded without words and turned to watch splinters of sun filter through the small leaves and angled branches above. They dotted a cobbled light trail to the edge of the river where a little girl had been playing a half an hour before. Her parents had redirected her there after her natural curiosity drew her to investigate what we were doing in our huddle in the shade of a few trees.

Discreet as we were, we must have appeared as a spectacle of some sort. That is, if anything sticks out in Sedona. The town is a hub of the unusual, what with vortex hikes and crystal shops and UFO-watching parties. While none of that was a draw for me, I was completely impressed with the grandeur of the land. It's a place of magnificent natural beauty. Cathedral Rock is one of the most photographed subjects in the U.S. Southwest, an utterly breathtaking area where brides and grooms in hiking shoes exchange their vows in a vast rock expanse turned wedding chapel.

The Cherokee medicine woman, Pamela Dancing Buffalo, was native to the region and knew this land intimately. Earlier in the day she told us that in long-ago maps of the area, Cathedral Rock was known as Courthouse Rock, and nearby Courthouse Butte was known as Church House Rock.

"Look at the pinnacle over there," she pointed up with her back to us at the trailhead. "Can you see how one rock appears to be the shape of a woman and the other a man, facing away from each other?"

Pamela turned to look at us. "There are actually two different ways the Native Americans tell the story about this place. They both begin the same way.

"It's said that long long ago, a man and woman were walking along the river, in the midst of an argument so heated and loud that they woke up a great serpent living in the river's bend. This is where the stories diverge. One myth holds that the serpent was so angry, it cast the man and woman up to the sky and turned them into rock.

"The other ending to the story is that the serpent awakened by the argument was very wise. The serpent told the man and woman that when two beings come together, they must do so in trust and love. They must honor their unique and sometimes opposite perspectives, but also their dependence on one another.

"So the wise serpent carved a reminder for the man and the woman into the cliffs, making it so they leaned on each other back to back. In this way, they'd always feel support and connection. But they faced different directions, because the man and woman should never forget they each had their own journey in life. And look at the very small rock next to them. Some people feel this represents the child who arrived as a result of their joining together.

"Of course, the second myth is why so many people come to Cathedral Rock to get married."

After Pamela's explanation, we began our hike upstream, with the intention of creating a ceremony together at a sacred spot near the notable serpent bend in the river.

Two miles later, we arrived and the group scattered to explore the pristine spot. Pamela and the mutual friend who introduced us settled under the grove of trees and motioned me over. "We'd like you to join us in setting up this ceremony," Pamela said.

"No, that's okay, this is your land, please lead the way." I politely declined. I was reluctant to join in, having just come from a caldera in the Tortolita Mountains of Tuscon where my catalyst medicine took on a rather volcanic expression. I was quite content to remain on the sidelines and be a spiritual tourist.

"But these are your folks, Pat." Pamela glanced toward the participants who came along for this second leg of the Arizona trip. "Please, please join me."

In spite of the hesitancy I felt, I agreed.

As we prepared, I bought my mesa to join hers. The mesa is a cloth bundle of sacred stones I carried as a part of my initiation into the practice of Andean medicine. It was a kind of mandala, used to configure and work with my internal world. I reached in and removed a stone that had called out to me from a river in Peru only weeks before. The stone had been carved by strong moving water for centuries—maybe longer—shaping it into a vessel. I filled its recess with a scented, alcohol-based water we often used in ceremony and set it alight. When the stone found me in Peru, it instructed me to allow my medicine of service to the world to flow from this cup.

I still felt uneasy, but I was willing.

As we gathered the group around the fire for our ceremony, Pamela shared what had occurred for her during meditation that morning. For more than a year, she'd been the keeper of two ancient artifacts—a serpent head and a tortoise shell—for a Native American tribe from Southern California. They were said to be three thousand years old. Pamela explained that a close friend asked her in the days before his death if she'd become the steward of the sacred relics. He instructed her to keep them safe until they were returned to their tribe. I forget whether Pamela told us why or how he had come by them himself, how or when the return of the artifacts would take place, or what Pamela's role was in keeping them.

"I haven't opened this pouch more than three times since these were entrusted to me," Pamela said as she carefully unwrapped the serpent head and tortoise shell and passed them in opposite directions around the circle. "This morning I received a message that you're a very special group. I was instructed to use these in ceremony with all of you, so you could receive the medicine they hold. The tortoise shell represents feminine energy, and the serpent head, masculine. To me, this exemplifies the lore of Cathedral Rock, a place where true joining can occur, bringing the masculine and feminine together in a cooperative dance, while appreciating difference."

The group moved into silence, palpable power, and possibility.

When the serpent head was handed to me, I placed it on top of my medicine bag of stones, and blew through it to transfer the invisible medicine it carried—metaphorically anchoring the wisdom and essence of the serpent head—into my bundle. I did the same with the tortoise shell when it reached me. The others followed my lead. It was indeed an honor to accept these ancient sacred relics in this way. When something enters the bundle of a medicine carrier, it becomes a part of every aspect of the self as well.

It was as if we became witnesses at our own weddings. And like the myth of Cathedral Rock that Pamela recounted earlier, something was growing from this joining, about to be born, evident in the third and smaller of the red carved rocks, which loomed overhead as the offspring of the larger two.

It was after this ceremony that she handed me the leather pouch and I prepared to go. But before leaving the magical site, I looked around one final time. It was hard to pull away from the beauty of this place.

A large and stubborn stone in the center of the river caught my eye. In stalwart protest, it seemed to be losing an age-old game with the insistent force of water. But if you paid close attention, you could hear delight calling out from under the stone's jagged edges. Upholding the rules of a secret partnership with the river, the rock seemed to cry in pleasure at being shimmed and chipped bit by bit, while simultaneously keeping up a façade of protest at the slow carving of this ancient water sculptor. It reminded me of my own hesitancy about joining Pamela as a co-facilitator of the ceremony. Even my vessel stone was like the rock I stared at now—its wounds carved so deeply by the river that it could be used as a cup to quench the thirst of others or, perhaps, hold an offering of fire.

The rock began to speak.

Things aren't always as they appear. While you can put your hand more easily through water than stone, everything has the capacity to become the more powerful force. Do not doubt the strength of what appears to be the weaker.

I had absolutely no idea what the rock was talking about, so I stood up.

Grasping the smooth skin of the leather pouch, which I held firmly upright in my hand, I left the river's edge and the group, walking back to Sylvia and Maya, whom I found spread on a blanket waiting for us to return. A condition with Maya's spine prevented her from taking the hike with the rest of us. Sylvia stayed to keep her company. I was excited to recreate the ceremony with them that we shared with Pamela.

When I rejoined my two friends, I knelt down on the blanket and took a good look at both of them. "Something pretty powerful happened up there," I said as I began untying the knot at the top of the leather pouch. "Pamela sent me ahead to recreate our ceremony with you." I reached in and pulled out the tortoise shell and placed it on the blanket we were sitting on. I reached back in for the serpent head, but ... *there was nothing in the bag. There was nothing in the bag. There was nothing in the bag.*

Sylvia and Maya saw the shock on my face. I quickly told them what appeared to be missing, as I looked around the blanket and the grass nearby to see if the serpent's head had somehow dropped out when I removed the tortoise shell. Surely we would've seen something fall onto the blanket. I shifted off my heels to sit stunned. Finally, I recounted the short history of the artifacts to Sylvia and Maya before moving into quiet.

I turned inward and listened, hearing this message: *It is exactly as it is supposed to be.*

I felt that as strongly as I've ever felt anything—until the next wave hit: *Get real, Pat. It seems you just lost a sacred three-thousand-year-old artifact.*

Yet there wasn't even a tiny ring of truth in it. No energy at all. Not a bit. The message was still clear: *It's perfect just the way it is*—even if I *had* somehow lost it.

It occurred to me that it was possible that just because something vanishes doesn't mean it's gone, like the sun that sets each night and seems to disappear.

My mind rewound the entire trek along the river to the blanket anyway.

It must've fallen out back under the grove of trees or somehow never got into the pouch in the first place. But Pamela never would have been so careless. She barely touched these artifacts herself. The leather strings were tied together. She handed it directly to me and it never tipped over. I had the pouch gripped in my hand upright the whole time. I was aware of the preciousness of the pouch as I was carrying it back. It was like a baby. It was tied tight when I just undid it. It couldn't have fallen out. Maya and Sylvia watched me untie the knot.

All of the machinations of the mind were in full gear, but they kept circling back to: *Everything is fine, perfect as it is, exactly how it's supposed to be.*

Fuck," I said aloud to Maya and Sylvia. "How am I ever gonna explain this to Pamela?"

I stood up, pacing a little, then walked over to an enormous tree. I sat at the base and breathed in its support, connecting my spine to hers. Its trunk was more than five times the width of me.

I remembered six or seven years ago, when a colleague of mine, who had passed away just a month earlier, told me I really needed to consider spending more time leaning my back against a tree. "Do you realize that you pour yourself so wholeheartedly into everything in front of you that you actually lean forward every time you speak? You don't have to do it all alone, you know. You need a good tree behind you." I found myself missing Ona, a little sorry that I was too mute to speak at the memorial fire we had for her, having just returned from the mountain trek in Peru that seemed to steal my tongue. She was with me now in the wind. I felt the tree at my back. My thoughts reeled, accelerating to the speed of light.

Maybe this is what happens when two powerful forces come together? Bliss is created for a moment as the two vanish into one. Then, just before the nothingness that is probably liberation, we become afraid we've permanently disappeared and we pop back into separation again ... and then spend our time either chasing bliss or becoming paralyzed by our growing fear of the dark. It's an utterly unamusing amusement-park ride of chills and thrills that goes on and on in a neverending loop.

"Pat, they're coming," Maya called over, startling me out of my merger with the tree.

I rose reluctantly and walked across the grass toward Pamela, as she and a few others emerged from the woods. When I reached her, I suggested she sit down on a bench nearby. As I told her what happened, I knelt down so we could see each other at eye level and said, "Pamela, I know how precious these artifacts are, but somehow, I think this was supposed to be."

She turned toward me and sharply retorted, "This was *not* supposed to happen." After a moment, she continued, "There will be consequences for this. These artifacts were entrusted to me for safekeeping and I breached that trust. But Pat, I don't want you to carry any guilt for this."

Truth be said, there wasn't a guilty bone in my whole body in that moment. But I could clearly hear her fear of the consequences and the guilt for having entrusted the precious relics to me, a member of another tribe, and unleashing an attachment Armageddon that recoiled at least three thousand years into the past. On the other hand, I trusted entirely what happened and knew somehow there was extraordinary blessing in it. It was the only thing I knew. But I couldn't avoid the pain before me. And the truth that what was Pamela's was also mine.

I'd have to join her in the pain, like the tree and Ona did with me a few minutes earlier, so she wouldn't have to carry it all alone ... so I didn't have to carry it all alone. While the group organized a kind of search-and-rescue mission for the serpent head, retracing two miles of steps back to the bend in the river, people began speaking in whispers. A black cloud descended over the group.

The circulating pain was now moving around me as well as in front of me.

Nothing is as it appears.

I could hear the echo of the voice of the lone rock standing strong against—and with—the toss of the rapids of the river up near where we had our ceremony. I remembered seeing the time-lapse chipping away of the rock as the water gained speed. I let the awareness of it accelerate my acceptance of the pain around me, as it turned to suffering.

I let the weaker force I perceived as the river upstream become the stronger force and allowed it to sweep me in a downward spiral, all the way into the great core of myself, a descending reach not unlike the roots of the enormous tree I'd just spent twenty minutes leaning against.

Apparently, I was about to get a Sedona vortex tour after all.

Outside of me, the Las Vegas-style wedding at Cathedral Rock quickly entered divorce court. No wonder the old maps of the place confused Courthouse Rock with Church House Rock.

Inside, I vanished into the suffering around me, trusting without thinking, merging without control, down into the great pit we're all afraid of when we cannot remember.

I had no choice but to descend into the abyss.

Chapter 25

Spiral Up and Fly to Liberty

Looking back, I'm unsure whether other words flanked the one, loud, emphatic "No!" that bolted like lightning out of the mouth of my friend and colleague, Damien, as he slammed his hand against the rental-car dashboard returning me in a rapid spiral up and out of the abyss.

At precisely the same moment, an enormous tractor-trailer roared by us in the left lane. Like it's said about a lightning strike, there was no time to count one-one-thousand, two-one-thousand, three-one-thousand, while waiting for the thunderclap to predict the distance of the bolt. There was no space between. The strike and clap occurred simultaneously, turning the air electric inside the car.

It reminded me of an incident that occurred fifteen years earlier during a workshop I attended. The program title was something like: "Finding Your Path of Sacred Service in the World." As it turned out, I didn't need to stay through the entire program to find my path. My path found me within the first half-hour.

There were maybe two hundred of us gathered on the pewless chapel floor of an old Jesuit novitiate turned yoga center.

The original workshop registration was low, so local community-service agencies were offered no-cost slots to fill the program. Apparently, finding one's path to sacred service wasn't trending widely at the time.

After a welcome from the presenters, we were asked to break into small groups and share with one another what drew us to attend.

When it came time for the noticeably awkward, cross-legged man to my left to introduce himself, his shoulders hunched and he rocked quietly back and forth on his tail-bone. A half-minute or so passed; other group members exchanged quizzical glances while waiting for him to speak. Still, the man was silent. I lifted my hand and gently rested it on his upper arm in a gesture of support, while looking down at the floor in front of me so he wouldn't feel pressured. "It's okay to let it out," I whispered softly.

Looking back, I realize any number of things could have been the catalyst to unleash what came next. Maybe the touch of my hand was too intimate; maybe the words I used gave him the simple permission he needed to release some kind of long-suppressed urge. Perhaps he was a client of one of the service agencies represented in the room and the scene was overwhelming for him. Whatever the cause, after a long breath in, the man let out the loudest blood-curdling scream I ever heard.

It was as if it traveled up from the bedrock beneath the foundation of the building and rocketed out of the top of his head, past the old chapel rafters and beyond to the Berkshire night. The entire room went quiet. Two hundred pairs of eyes turned to our small breakout group to view this man's wide O mouth and my lightning-rod hand affixed to his arm. I was unable to move, as if the current from some live wire were electrocuting me. After what seemed like an eternity, but was probably only fifteen seconds, he stopped. I let go of his arm and returned it to my lap.

I tried to look unaffected, but I was shaken to my core. Shaken awake.

As the aftershock abated, soft conversations began to resume in the other small circles. No one came over to say, "Sir, are you all right?" Neither did anyone in our little circle. It was treated as a passing storm.

I have no exact recollection of what happened next, though I'm pretty sure he introduced himself as if nothing at all unusual had just taken place. All I remember is that I felt increasingly uneasy through the night and, after having bouts of dizziness at breakfast, decided to leave. I knew my discomfort was a kind of excuse, but I was also sure I wanted to run as far away from possible from what was in that room.

I calculated hundreds of other possible places in the yoga center where this man could have sat. But he ended up next to me. Having spent many years working professionally with people with disabilities, it wasn't unusual to find myself as a kind of safety magnet for people who navigated the world differently from mainstream norms. I was the person who could evoke a shy, sideways smile from the avoidant gaze of someone with autism or a stranger hug from a child with Down's Syndrome in the grocery store as if I were a long lost relative. But this … this was in a category all of its own.

The only way I could describe it to the few people I told when I got home was that I felt as if I'd been struck by lightning. It took me a while to realize that it was a kind of gateway into, as the curriculum title aptly stated, "My Path of Sacred Service in the World. " In little more than a year, the room where that storm took place would become the center of an unfolding chapter of my life.

There, I received my certification to teach yoga after thirty days of intensive training. Three or four years later, I was co-teaching a neo-shamanic healing program, after having answered a call to what became my life's work, passing on initiations to others that I received from descendants of the Inkas. They were the wisdom keepers of the northern Andes, a high-mountain lineage of sages who were purportedly called to their work by being struck by lightning—the real kind.

But perhaps the cross-legged man wasn't the only source of voltage and I wasn't any special initiate. Maybe we all carried a spark within which awaited various and ordinary circumstances to set it alight. But for certain, that room was a metaphoric match for me, pun intended. It awakened the synthesis of my deep Catholic roots, the depth I found in the study and practice of yoga and cursory Buddhist leanings, and the healing traditions and wisdom teachings transmuted from an ancient indigenous culture into contemporary form.

That event so long ago was linked to this moment in the rental car by the same impulse to run away, but was also tied as a foreshadow of a new cycle about to begin.

Damien and I had left Sedona before dawn. Somewhere around Campe Verde, Arizona, while the morning sky glowed yellow-pink in the rear-view mirror, I announced my resignation as a professional catalyst.

"I'm really done, Damien. I can't do it anymore. It's waaay too much," I said, choking back sobs. "I'm tired of being a walking spark for things around me to ignite. I feel like I left the rocks around Sedona redder and hotter than I found them. I'm burned out. It's all too powerful. I'm calling it quits. I absolutely *hate* being a catalyst."

After ten days in the hot desert, I'd left more than a few fires burning on the trails behind me. It was as if the work were suddenly operating on a different level. In the past year, it seemed I was already in the midst of a personal electrical upgrade from 100 to 200 amps. But after visiting Peru not long before Sedona, something radically changed. Apparently, I didn't receive the metaphorical memo that a merger with the United Illuminating Company was imminent. And not the one that provided the State of Connecticut with electrical service.

This refusal was my invitation for an uncharacteristic "No!" from Damien, punctuated by a palm hitting the dash. Unlike the first in my series of pseudo-electric events, this storm was a direct hit and, unlike the first in my series of pseudo-electric events, I wasn't running away from the call.

"Oh, I guess you're right," I said matter-of-factly, having been instantly jolted up from the abyss. I moved from pure melodrama to radical acceptance in one scorched second. We rode in silence the rest of the way to the Phoenix airport. During the drive, my memory floated back to the morning I left the yoga center many years before.

I remembered explaining to the yogi clerk behind the front desk that I wasn't feeling well and while disappointed, I wasn't going to be able to finish the workshop about finding my path to sacred service. Truth be told, I was secretly hoping for sympathy and a refund, though I knew it wasn't the center's policy.

"I know what you mean," he offered nonchalantly,

barely looking up from his paperwork. "I've been there before. It's like wanting the shiny blue bike to be under the tree on Christmas morning and what you get instead is the Encyclopedia Britannica." It was as if he could read the fact that I was fleeing and being sick was an excuse.

I don't know how he saw my gaze turn to the tiny cards in the long rectangular box sitting atop the reception station, because he still seemed preoccupied with whatever he was working on. "Good idea. Yeah. Why don't you take one of those before you leave? It may give you a little perspective," he said.

Each seemed to have a phrase printed on it. I shuffled my fingers through and picked one out. The one I chose read: *The Only Way Out Is Through.*

Fifteen years later, as I continued the drive in silence to the airport, I received an upgrade to the original message: There Is No Way Out. Out Is In and In Is Out.

By the time I returned the rental car and parted company with Damien to get on our separate flights, a whole lifetime had passed. I was more than ready to rise from the fiery desert tarmac of Phoenix as a phoenix myself. The metaphor made me chuckle.

I was one of the last to board. As I stepped onto the airplane bound for Newark Liberty International Airport, a flight attendant was encouraging passengers to raise their hands to signal the location of nearby empty seats. There were only a few. But it wasn't the show of hands that called me to my seat. It was the shriek of a crying baby from the back that got my attention.

Ah, the sound of new life. I knew what I had to do. I needed to find a seat as close to the screaming baby as I could.

So down the narrow aisle I went with my backpack,

edging around bustling bodies stuffing overhead compart-
ments with carry-on baggage. Just a few seats up from the
back galley and restrooms and across the aisle from the
howling was a single empty seat. I excused myself to get past
a pleasant sixty-something couple and wedged down next
to the window. I was oddly comforted by the thrash and
wail from the distressed or hungry baby across the aisle. As
I settled in, the friendly woman next to me turned and said:
"We sat here because we love babies. We have grandchildren
of our own. It's *the sound of new life*."

Out Is In and In Is Out, all right.

How curious—two sets of travelers who deliberately
sat *next* to a crying child on a plane, when most passengers
would have opted for the opposite. She was the immediate
outer manifestation of my inner impulse.

Marcie, the woman in the middle seat, and her husband Mark were traveling to New Jersey for the funeral of
his sister's husband. Mostly when I fly, I plug in my headset,
read a book, work on my laptop, or take a nap. I rarely
engage with a fellow passenger with more than a smile and
a few polite words. But this was already no ordinary flight.
And Marcie was no ordinary passenger. The plane barely
began to taxi before the baby across the aisle settled and
was asleep.

"So what brought you to Phoenix?" Marcie inquired in
a way only a true extrovert would.

"Well," I paused, while making a conscious decision
to tell the truth rather than make up a superficial story. "I
wasn't in Phoenix. I was leading a personal-growth retreat
down in Tucson, then drove to Sedona with some of the
folks who attended."

"Really. Who were the people? Were they from Arizona?" she asked. At this point, I knew that the in-flight-magazine crossword puzzle was not in my future.

"It was a combination of Native American tribal leaders, some locals, and other people from my area who flew out to be there. We made up our own kind of diverse tribe, I guess." I edited out the parts about leaving several metaphoric fires burning behind me and didn't talk in depth about what happened to me at Cathedral Rock when the three-thousand-year-old relic disappeared and I began a three-day downward spiral through centuries of stories of human suffering and separation, while actually experiencing each of them as mine.

I let go of my stranger filter and guard and gave in to Marcie's probing questions, not caring that she might consider me crazy. I recounted a few of the truths about my trip and its mix of richness and pain. Our conversation began to anchor around what constitutes tribe, collective, or family. We talked about competition and in-fighting, envy, fear, righteousness, and of course, love.

It turned out that tribe was the perfect part of the tale on which to focus. After answering many of Marcie's questions and conversing about my work, she began to share her own story.

"I can really relate to all that. Mark and I are both devout Catholics. Our son married a Mormon. It's raised challenges for me as a mom, a mother-in-law, and a grandmother. I feel like we've run into the same thing you're talking about. It's this sense of no longer belonging. Sometimes I feel ostracized by my own flesh and blood."

It seemed fated that Marcie and I would speak for the entire duration of the cross-country flight. In the next four and a half hours, I shared with her the deep regard I held for my Catholic roots and how they were enriched, rather than undermined, by my spiritual explorations of the past thirty years. I rarely talked about it; I'd often run into skepticism from some in the Christian faith about Earth-based wisdom and its pagan roots. But it didn't seem to set off any devil-alarm in Marcie. Far from it.

I shared how the death and resurrection story seemed to chase the group I was with in Sedona all over the desert. We talked about religious tribes and colonization and intolerance, all of the subjects that passed through me as a relived experience in the downward spiral of the past three days before I had rejected my own call and recommitted to it again an instant later.

About midway between Phoenix and Newark, Marcie went deeply into her story about her relationship with her daughter-in-law. Before long, we were working together to retell her story as a healing engagement, rather than a divisive struggle.

Then, Marcie's husband Mark, who seemed oblivious to our conversation of the past couple of hours, leaned past his tray table and the movie on his iPad to look over at me.

"I hope you don't mind, but I just wanted to say, you should get the work you do out there in the world. I heard you tell Marcie you want to write a book. I really think you should do it. I know someone who might be able to help you."

Mark had apparently been listening to Marcie and me talk about the power of how we tell our stories. He must have overheard my longing to share the stories of my clients with others and the fact that my schedule was too full with family and work obligations to tackle the task.

Conventional wisdom said you needed to take a sabbatical to write, but that didn't seem to account for the time or financial resources needed to do it, which I didn't have. It was completely impractical.

So when Mark punctuated his words by passing me the business card of an author and owner of a Las Vegas marketing and communications company, I listened.

The great gamble was about to begin.

"You may want to call this man. Talk to him. Maybe there's a way he can help you publish your stories." Repositioning the ear bud of his headset back into his ear, he settled back to watch his movie.

Before landing in Newark, Marcie asked me if she could read me a passage from a book that was in the bag stowed below the seat in front of her. It was a compilation of prayers, one for every day of the year. The last verse of the prayer for October 30 was this: *When you step back into the mainstream of life, strain to hear those glorious bells: I am with you, I am with you, I am with you.*

My eyes welled with tears. The universal love and intelligence, the living wisdom, the great magic that we refer to by many more names seemed everywhere, in everything and everyone.

When it was finally our turn in the back to deplane, I glanced over and made eye contact with the now-bundled baby who called me to my seat. I gave him, or maybe her, one of those silly scrunched-face smiles we reserve for tiny ones. I got a wide and mostly toothless grin back in return. Mark and I shook hands. Marcie and I hugged. As they continued on to reunite with their own tribe at the memorial service, I was off to re-commit to being a catalyst and to re-birth the abandoned idea of writing a book.

There was no space between Death and Resurrection. In the era of United Illuminating, it was coincident.

I stepped out the plane door and walked through the jetway. When I reached the terminal, I smiled when I read the Newark airport greeting sign in front of me:

Welcome to Liberty.

Epilogue
Where They Are Now

Emily, who deepened my capacity to trust what appears within and in front of me, literally reunited with her Greater Core several years after our first session, when she passed away not long after her housebound husband. I was privileged to be at both their deathbeds, helping them to trust the journey beyond this life.

Along with other Andean paqos, Don Mariano Quispe Flores continues to travel to initiate others into the ancient teachings of wisdom and heart of his vanishing culture, assuring its legacy lives on.

Bernadette, whose brother died of AIDS, brought the gifts of the new vision she received in the group experience in New Jersey to her extended family, where appreciation for the beauty of our unique and intertwined roles in life rippled wider in love. She remains peacefully free from the twenty-five-year guilt associated with not holding her brother at the time of his passing.

Sue continues to blow things out of proportion with little effort in a wonderful way, most effects subtle rather than direct. I reached her in San Francisco as she was on a multi-destination trip, having expanded her concert-ticket karma to airline-ticket karma by simply volunteering to step off overbooked flights. This has led to more time with her wide social circle and aging parents who live at a distance. Like her photo with Sir Paul, she feels wrapped in the arms of love more than ever.

Daniel, the bright and precocious ten-year-old who informed my coaching practice by helping me to better understand the mission of a true superhero, is now a young teen with a passion for animation. His online animatic creation to the song "Wait For It" from the Broadway show *Hamilton* has nearly 42,000 hits on You Tube.

By shifting the way the story of his father's demand to get a job or leave home lived in him, artist Tebbe Kevin Davis's work is now in greater market demand. When we spoke last, he'd just received four large commissions from a realtor who, interestingly, asked Tebbe to paint beautiful keepsakes for his clients who were leaving their homes. Please browse his gallery at www.tebbedavis.com.

Jackie continues with her practice of accepting that "You Can't Always Get What You Want," despite the very real, human protests that often come when we get what we don't want. In the two years after experiencing relief that her cancer didn't recur, she made the courageous decision to leave a marriage she initially *didn't want* to let go of. In doing so, Jackie reports that she, her ex-husband, and her children are enjoying a more loving relationship as a family who now live in two separate homes.

☙

Shortly after our session, Kevin and Lisa bought a home they truly love in Connecticut. When I contacted her to ask how they were doing, They'd just returned home after a harrowing plane flight from the west coast with two kids in tow. Lisa reports she continues to trust that grand leaps to the idyllic and exotic (like moving to Bali) are sometimes wisely postponed in favor of what's right in plain sight. While world travel and relocation still pend as a dream, Kevin and Lisa are also trusting the timing, for the time being, in their Connecticut dream home.

Sandy, who lost the bright light of her mentor to cancer and discovered the value of the dim bulb, recently accepted an early retirement from her corporate job to devote herself to her new consulting business, www.thealchemyleaders. com. She reports that her life and energy as a successful coach moved into a more refined "conscious calibration" as she released her grip on brightness, realized the beauty of the dusky dark, and recognized that the light never totally disappears.

After navigating the uncertain and following the stars, young Grace returned to California, accepted an opportunity to become a nanny, and helped her aunt care for her grandmother. This led her to discover a passion for caregiving and an interest in alternative healing. She plans to move with friends to Santa Cruz, California, where she'll attend herbology school.

Genevieve had a great year of challenge and adventure at early college in semi-rural western Massachusetts. She reports the odd couple of I'm Mature and Amateur in her continue to live on in her decision to transfer to a much larger college where her academic and theater interests can ripen her talents and she can live closer to New York City, where the fun and playful remain vibrantly alive for her.

Ness continues to dive deep for the gold in the lake of her inner world with greater love and acceptance. She has found more love in the surface world as a result.

Matthew practices aiming with love to reach new levels of Oscar-worthy recognition, using the gift his deceased brother-in-law gave him in our session. While he and his own brother have not yet resumed contact, he continues to trust the separation and is certain they'll be reunited at the right moment for both of them. Matthew's current targets include the recent release of a CD of sacred chants and opening a farm-to-table café near his home in upstate New York.

Peter, the retired firefighter, remains as wise as ever. He continues to accept fluctuations in his health without compromising his dreams and the possibilities for leading a full and vibrant life. As he shared the story of the recent loss of his beloved seventeen-year-old Jack Russell terrier, and the legacy this close four-legged friend left him for life, I couldn't help but hear the connection to our session where I suggested Peter consider befriending death as his trusted partner and ally. It seems his furry companion, who made ordinary trips to the hardware store experiences of unconditional love, became the embodiment of this invisible friendship that still walks by his side.

Chris, who shattered the sphere in the gazebo, and Sara, whom he asked to step next to him as he did, were married for real two months later—at dawn on the spring equinox on the mountain where they fell in love during class. I had the great privilege of being the officiant of their ceremony.

Christine, my childhood friend whose home was leveled by the tornado and was dealing with the twisting winds of unemployment, was hired for a job she's come to love, after the perfect amount of time out of work to accomplish even more home-improvement projects. In the early autumn after our call recounted in her chapter, a hurricane was reported to be heading toward the shoreline community of her small Florida vacation home, where it was expected to make landfall. I called her as soon as I heard the news and found her upbeat. "Who gets to go through something like this twice in one lifetime?" she laughed, completely unalarmed, even amused by the reports in a "Surrender Dorothy" kind of way. This time, the storm turned to the north and only grazed her town, sparing her house from damage.

Caron was transferred to the forensic unit of a state mental-health facility after the judge who heard his case found him not guilty for reasons of insanity. He spent fourteen months awaiting this decision in prison and likely set a record for being the inmate most visited by friends and family members. Leah, his mom, has only seen him in court appearances, but speaks to him on the phone when he calls, and was delighted to get an "I love you" from him recently. He and I continue to exchange raps via mail.

The woman with cerebral palsey, who wept a lake of tears into the sand of the desert, built a pool off the master bath of her home in the two years following the Arizona retreat. She, and her metaphoric mermaid tail that signifies her unique and beautiful difference, swims daily in the color-fully painted cinderblock addition, replete with a swim-up

Mexican folk-art exhibit and a mermaid shrine. Now retired and unstopped by challenge or the Arizona heat, she plans to have a pond dug into her front yard that will house a rare kind of fish. It will be large enough so she can submerge herself alongside them. One pool for her fellow humans, the other for her fellow fish.

After the Arizona retreat where the Red Fire Priest fell to Mother Earth, I didn't hear from him. He couldn't look me in the eye the day I left, still reeling from the vulnerability of being stripped naked— and my provocative role in it. It was eighteen months before he reached out with this message: "How do you properly thank someone who taught you how to love again?"

In the months after this acknowledgment, his Red Fire tribe was recognized by and reunited with the Cherokee Nation after more than three hundred years of separation. He was called to Oklahoma where he was awarded the Cherokee Patriot Medal of Honor and designated as a spiritual leader for his people. Members of the Oklahoma tribe are scheduled to come to the Valley of the Seven Sisters in Arizona to become reacquainted with the old ways and teachings of the Red Fire, the warrior path.

He told me that when he was sent to Vietnam, his tribe held a ceremony that "stripped him of his humanity," so he could participate in war. However, his humanity was never returned to him, as was the custom in the old culture when a warrior came home from battle. He acknowledged that when he fell to lie on Her, he was reawakened to his vulnerability, his humanity, and his ability to love again. It was the ceremony for which he'd waited almost fifty years.

I contacted Pamela Dancing Buffalo, our unofficial guide at Cathedral Rock, explaining that I was writing an account of our experience in Sedona. I asked if she might share the story of her journey after the serpent head was lost and what occurred with the California tribe to whom the relic belonged. I received a warm and gracious wish for good luck, but no further information was shared.

A couple of months after the events of Cathedral Rock, Damien and I were visiting together when another electric moment occurred between us while working with our medicine bundles on the floor of my office. Thinking about what happened in Sedona, I brought out a tortoise shell I had found years before in a box of items salvaged through my husband's business. While it sat on the floor between us, Damien casually picked up a meteor from my mesa, my medicine bundle of stones, and as if dropping the final—and missing—puzzle piece in place, he sat the piece of moldavite in a small notch on the front of the shell. I never realized a serpent and a turtle-head looked the same. In that moment I understood the significance of what occurred at Cathedral Rock, the place where duality and singularity met: Just because something vanishes doesn't mean it's gone. Like the turtle's head, it tucks away into the comfort of totality to emerge again another day.

As for Marcie and Mark, I never saw or spoke to them again after our flight to Liberty, but I did contact the writing coach Mark recommended in Las Vegas. You're now drinking from the last lake of words that were once only a mirage in the desert walk of writing.

Now, it's all simply magic in plain sight.

Acknowledgements
(and Deep Bows)

To the loving community of students and clients who entrusted me with their stories so others might benefit, I bow to you.

To Lucia Barretti, who accompanied me, step-by-step, through the walk in the desert that was the writing process, and for what you *saw* on the Main Chapel steps in 1993 that set it all in motion.

To Brian Rouff and Bob Burris of Imagine Communications in Las Vegas for your confidence in the big gamble this project was for me, and for your wisdom and guidance on this journey, which made a great effort (nearly) effortless. You allowed me to realize that the only ghostwriter I needed for the project all along was the *Holy Ghost*writer in me.

To Deke Castleman who brought immense support and encouragement, in addition to skillful editing, to these words, and made the stories flow so well.

To Rob Cole and Joan Sutherland, for the beautiful poetry you so generously contributed.

To David Mensah, for the thousands of hours of logged conversation which prepared the way, as well as a deep bow for performing the ultimate magic trick that ultimately supported my ability to complete this leg of the great journey as the pilot and navigator I needed to be.

To those friends who generously offered their many gifts, from good questions to chapter feedback, from author care to financial help, and various kinds of other support, I am forever grateful: Judith Hackman, Deborah and Charles Weber, Angela Amendola, Deb Robinson, Christopher Zurcher, Kimberley Windbiel, Jerry Wistrom, Sue Neufeld, Pat Hillen, book club members, and the many more I can't list here who offered many tiny encouragements with huge impact. You've made all the difference in the world.

To my kind and loving husband Joe, and children Lia, Kyla, and Lucas, I love you all more than words can ever tell.

To the crying baby on the Southwest Flight from Phoenix to Newark, thank you for being hungry, having a dirty diaper, or meeting me on some mystical plane of synchronicity that I could've so easily overlooked.

Without you, this book might never have come to be.

About the Author

Patricia (Pat) Heavren is an educator, coach, energy-medicine practitioner, workshop facilitator, and trained mediator. She worked for more than twenty years in the executive management of human-services organizations and holds a Master's degree in the field.

Pat is also a healer, a label she uses only by the following definition: assisting individuals, couples, and groups to remember the natural, immense, and unknowable source of intelligence within them, all around them, and especially right in front of them.

Her office is in Woodbridge, Connecticut, though she works with clients via phone and Skype internationally. She's adjunct faculty with The Graduate Institute in Bethany, Conn., and has taught programs in the U.S., Canada, and Latin America. She had the immense privilege of being senior teaching faculty with The Four Winds Society, where she completed her initial training.

Pat is blessed with a husband, three children, and an extraordinary tribe of friends.

She can be reached for private sessions at info@living-wisdom.guru